Palgrave Studies in Cyberpsychology

Series Editor
Jens Binder
Nottingham Trent University
Nottingham, UK

Palgrave Studies in Cyberpsychology aims to foster and to chart the scope of research driven by a psychological understanding of the effects of the 'new technology' that is shaping our world after the digital revolution. The series takes an inclusive approach and considers all aspects of human behaviours and experiential states in relation to digital technologies, to the Internet, and to virtual environments. As such, Cyberpsychology reaches out to several neighbouring disciplines, from Human-Computer Interaction to Media and Communication Studies. A core question underpinning the series concerns the actual psychological novelty of new technology. To what extent do we need to expand conventional theories and models to account for cyberpsychological phenomena? At which points is the ubiquitous digitisation of our everyday lives shifting the focus of research questions and research needs? Where do we see implications for our psychological functioning that are likely to outlast shortlived fashions in technology use?

Linda K. Kaye

The Psychology of Emoji Processing

Linda K. Kaye
Department of Psychology
Edge Hill University
Ormskirk, UK

ISSN 2946-2754   ISSN 2946-2762   (electronic)
Palgrave Studies in Cyberpsychology
ISBN 978-3-031-75112-7   ISBN 978-3-031-75113-4   (eBook)
https://doi.org/10.1007/978-3-031-75113-4

This Palgrave Macmillan imprint is published by the registered company Springer Nature Switzerland AG.
The registered company address is: Gewerbestrasse 11, 6330 Cham, Switzerland

If disposing of this product, please recycle the paper.

CONTENTS

LIST OF FIGURES

LIST OF TABLES

CHAPTER 1

Introduction

Abstract Chapter 1 introduces the pervasiveness of emoji in twenty-first-century society and indicates the scholarly interest that has been afforded to them. Chapter 1 provides a brief overview of key insights on the psychological study of emoji in broad terms and how these help us answer key questions about emoji. Chapter 1 provides a summary of how scholars have studied emoji in respect of emotion, cognition and behaviour to illustrate how these are widely distributed across disciplines, making the synthesis of the literature rather challenging. This chapter concludes with a summary of how each chapter helps the reader navigate the question about how we process emoji through conceptual, theoretical and methodological lenses.

Keywords Emoji • Computer-mediated communication • Information processing • Emotion • Cognition • Behaviour

Emoji are a popular and persuasive part of twenty-first century communication. Emoji themselves are highly diverse and can represent faces depicting various emotions, as well depict objects, symbols or actions. Within this book, when I refer to "emoji", this will be making reference to facial emoji which depict emotion (e.g., happy face, angry face) unless otherwise specified. It is worth noting also the term "emoji" can refer to both the

L. K. Kaye, *The Psychology of Emoji Processing*, Palgrave
Studies in Cyberpsychology,
https://doi.org/10.1007/978-3-031-75113-4_1

1

singular and the plural and so I use this term in both these respects throughout this book.

Emoji have fascinated scholars over the last few decades, which is evidenced from published work which extends across a wide range of disciplines including communication studies, media studies, computer science, digital humanities, semiotics, sociology and psychology. As a result, there is extensive academic literature on the study of emoji, which broadly helps us understand their role both on an individual level and societal level. At a societal level, scholars tend to focus on the symbolic relevance of emoji in social movements and discourse. At an individual level, and perhaps where the majority of psychological study is focused, this has helped us understand a wide range of issues. These include the role of emoji in emotional and sentimental communication, social or interpersonal processing, their role as paralinguistic or non-verbal cues, how they relate to semantic and lexical processing and their relationship to psychological characteristics of users such as personality traits.

Irrespective of the focus of study, emoji are broadly considered by scholars as a part of communication, most notably as a form of computer-mediated communication (CMC). However, divergence in opinions become evident when discussions are raised about the specific functions of emoji within communication. That is, are these part of emotional expression, part of semantic or lexical structures or are they simply serving as social/interpersonal signals?

It is pertinent to apply principles from communication to understand their affordances both from the sender's and receiver's perspective. A large majority of work as well as public discourse on emoji tends to focus on the sender, and ask questions such as who uses emoji, and how do emoji help us communicate effectively. However, there is relatively much less on the receiver perspective. That is, how emoji are actually processed, interpreted and/or responded to by receivers. Within the work which has been done from this perspective, this tends to focus more on the labels we use to interpret what different emoji mean and how we use them in judgement-making of others. However, there remain rather fundamental questions to answer about the receiver's perspective such as, do we actually process emoji emotionally? Or put another way, are emoji emotional? This requires a much more extensive exploration of the various processes and affordances which receivers experience with emoji and warrants some oversight in the literature.

This forms a key purpose of this book. Within this, I consolidate the existing literature on these issues to help you navigate the evidence to date regarding how we, as receivers, process emoji. To do this, I walk through the various approaches, theoretical frameworks and methods which have been used by researchers in this field and outline how this is helping answer questions such as:

- Can emoji support language comprehension?
- Are facial emoji emotional?
- Do we process emoji in the same way as faces?

Each of these draws on different conceptual and methodological approaches and within this book, I provide a review of these approaches to navigate you towards understanding the psychological study of emoji processing. Whilst this book is primarily focused on the receivers' perspective of emoji, it should be recognised that users will more often than not also embody the sender role within communicative exchanges. As such, we should acknowledge that the receiver's interpretation or processing of emoji is likely to be influenced by the way in which they use them as a sender. This is relevant to consider when reviewing the various perspectives introduced within this book, whereby we should not infer full separation between sender and receiver perspectives in our understanding of emoji processing.

WHAT DO WE MEAN BY "PROCESSING"?

Perhaps one of the fundamental questions to establish before going any further is what we actually mean by the term "processing". Indeed, this might often be used differently in different sub-discipline areas. Broadly speaking, "processing" (or information processing) is a term which is most commonly used within cognitive psychology, which perhaps immediately biases the focus of this issue towards perspectives and paradigms aligned to cognitive science over other psychological sub-disciplines. That being said, this provides a relatively strong basis to explain various aspects and characteristics of processing, such as the nature of attentional and perceptual processes and resources used, encoding and decoding of emoji information, connection to conceptual information in semantic memory, and the role of sensorimotor systems for interpreting and responding to emoji information. In relation to the study of emoji, some of the pertinent questions which an information processing approach might help address include:

- Do we process emoji consciously or subconsciously?
- What visual features of emoji and strategies do we use in emotion recognition?
- Are emoji linked to emotion concepts represented in semantic memory?

Whilst the term "processing" has strong connotations to cognitive psychology, this may also relate to wider psychological areas such as social cognition and interpersonal processing. As such, this can help answer questions such as:

- To what extent do people use emoji as cues for making personality impressions of others?
- When used in health communication, do emoji promote healthy attitudes and behaviour in receivers?

Within this book, I use the term "processing" to broadly refer to the way receivers interpret and/or respond to emoji, which may represent mechanisms at both a conscious and sub-conscious level.

How Have Psychologists Studied Emoji Processing?

Within the study of human psychology, we broadly are concerned with the human experience in the ways we function emotionally, cognitively and behaviourally. Interestingly, the scientific study of emoji has somewhat found itself situated in each of these to some extent or other, but not through any obvious coordinated thinking across scholars in the field. As such, the study of emoji currently sits across a variety of different subdiscipline silos, without much synergy or oversight on how these insights intersect to more broadly help us know how we actually process emoji. For example, Table 1.1 provides a general summary of insights across these somewhat disparate areas.

As you can see from Table 1.1, these exist in different disciplinary mindsets and methods which are not best placed to collectively help us really know the processing of emoji. Within this book, I take on this

Table 1.1 Summary of disciplinary approaches to the study of emoji

Facet of human psychology	Discipline/sub-discipline	Psychological constructs/processes	Indicative insights
Emotion	Affective science	Mood	How do we use emoji to represent/express mood? Are emoji valid indicators of mood?
	Consumer marketing/behaviour	Sentiment	Can emoji be a valid way to measure sentiment associated with products or experiences?
	Cognitive neuroscience/Affective science	Emotion recognition/detection	If emotions derived from emoji are processed in an equivalent way to faces, then the neurological processes should operate in an equivalent way.
Cognitive	Cognitive science	(Affective) Priming	If emoji share the equivalent emotion concept or valence to accompanying words, these could be used as affective primes to aid memory encoding of words with equivalent valence.
	Psycholinguistics	Semantic processing, semantic violation, lexical processing	If emoji share the equivalent emotion concept or valence to accompanying words/sentences, incongruent pairings would inhibit word processing and congruent pairings would facilitate processing.
	Psycholinguistics	Semantic binding	If emoji share semantic representations with accompanying words/sentences, their presence should support semantic binding processes.
	Psycholinguistics	Word/sentence comprehension and memory	If emoji share the equivalent emotion concept or valence to accompanying words/sentences, incongruent pairings would inhibit comprehension and/or memory recall and congruent pairings would facilitate this.
	Cognitive science	Embodied cognition/Grounded cognition	If concepts represented in emoji correspond to emotion concepts within conceptual thought, they should operate in equivalent ways to other emotional stimuli. If emoji valence shares the same directional value of concurrently presented sensory features of stimuli (visual positioning of stimuli, size of stimuli, auditory pitch), this should strengthen sensory signals and support conceptual integration. Thus congruence in the directional value should elicit more effective/efficient processing of emoji stimuli.

(continued)

Table 1.1   (continued)

Facet of human psychology	Discipline/ sub-discipline	Psychological constructs/processes	Indicative insights
	Vision science/ social neuroscience	Visual (face) processing	Eye gaze behaviour (visual search, identification of regions of interest, attentional vigilance via eye-tracking) can help us understand what facial features and/or task demands are relevant for how we process emoji faces (akin or otherwise to faces).
	Social neuroscience	Attentional bias/ vigilance	Eye gaze behaviour (visual search, identification of regions of interest via eye-tracking) and Dot Probe paradigms can help us understand how we might attend to emoji depicting specific types of emotion (akin to whether fearful/angry faces elicit greater attentional vigilance).
	Communication/ CMC	Multimodality and paralinguistics	To what extent do emoji function in an equivalent way to gestural communication to support receivers' interpretation of messages?
Behavioural	Cognitive (neuro) science/ behavioural neuroscience	Behavioural activation and avoidance	Do emoji as symbols of positive or negative emotions elicit action or avoidance tendencies and responses, as might be expected from their emotional counterparts?
	Social Psychology	Attitudes and behavioural intention, persuasion	What are the communicational functions of emoji to encourage behavioural outcomes?
	Social psychology/ personality psychology	Interpersonal perceptions	How receivers make interpersonal judgements of senders (e.g., warmth, personality, etc.) based on emoji use, type of emoji and so on.

challenge by taking an oversight of these insights to synthesise the state of play of how we process emoji.

Chapter 2 elaborates on the summary in Table 1.1 to provide a comprehensive review of the range of conceptual approaches which have been afforded to this issue, and what insights these have brought about. This includes conceptual approaches such as face processing, psycholinguistics, embodied/grounded cognition, emotion recognition/detection, affective experiences and interpersonal processing. This provides an overview of the main principles of these approaches, the types of research questions these approaches have addressed and the relevant insights gained.

Following this, Chap. 3 focuses more specifically on the value of specific theoretical frameworks which might be best suited to understand key mechanisms of specific elements of processes in the psychological study of emoji. This is distinctive from Chap. 2 in respect of identifying specific theories which might fit within these broader approaches to explain how the features of these theoretical frameworks might be operationalised within research to address certain research questions and used within certain paradigms. This includes those relating to the emotional functions of emoji:

Associative-Propositional Evaluation model (Gawronski & Bodenhausen, 2006, 2007), Broaden-and-Build theory (Fredrickson, 1998), and Reinforcement sensitivity theory (Gray, 1982, 1987). Cognitive processing includes Conceptual Metaphor Theory (Lakoff & Johnson, 1980), Perceptual Symbol Systems Framework (Barsalou, 1999), Dual Coding Model (Paivio, 1971), Sensory-semantic model (Nelson, 1979) and Prototypical Model of Picture and Word Processing (Snodgrass, 1980). Finally, interpersonal perspectives include Realistic Accuracy Model (Funder, 1995, 1999), Social Information Processing Theory (Walther, 1992), Emotion as Social Information (Van Kleef, 2009), Media Richness Theory (Daft & Lengel, 1986), Media Naturalness Theory (Kock, 2005, 2011), Channel Expansion Theory (Carlson & Zmud, 1999) and Elaboration Likelihood Model (Petty & Cacioppo, 1986). I argue that outlining the relevance of these various theoretical frameworks can support scholars in this field establish stronger theoretical underpinning for developing research questions, aligned to specific discipline traditions and paradigms.

Chapter 4 moves away from the conceptual and towards the methodological. Within this chapter, I review the range of methodological paradigms and measurements which have been used or could be relevant to the psychological study of emoji processing. This includes eye-tracking, Spatial stroop tasks, Lexical decision tasks, Dot probe tasks, Go/No-Go tasks, Approach-Avoidance tasks, memory retrieval tasks, perception scales and neurological measures such as EEG. Within this, I will outline the various measured outcomes associated with these methods, such as accuracy and latency of emotion recognition, semantic categorisation, approach-avoidance response, valence evaluation, attentional vigilance, word recall/comprehension, personality perceptions, judgement accuracy, message perceptions and attitudes/behavioural intentions.

Finally, Chap. 5 represents the conclusion, in which I will synthesise the key learning and take-home points from the respective chapters of the book and articulate an informed judgement about the state of play and future opportunities for the psychological study of emoji processing. Within this, I present my Emoji Research Toolkit as a practical tool to structure the research planning process for those seeking to develop programmes of research in this field.

References

Barsalou, L. W. (1999). Perceptual symbol systems. *Behavioral and Brain Sciences, 22,* 577–660. https://doi.org/10.1017/s0140525x99002149

Carlson, J. R., & Zmud, R. W. (1999). Channel expansion theory and the experiential nature of media richness perceptions. *Academy of Management Journal, 42*(2), 153–170. https://doi.org/10.2307/257090

Daft, R. L., & Lengel, R. H. (1986). Organizational information requirements, media richness and structural design. *Management Science, 32*(5), 554–571. https://doi.org/10.1287/mnsc.32.5.554

Fredrickson, B. L. (1998). What good are positive emotions? *Review of General Psychology, 2,* 300–319. https://doi.org/10.1037/1089-2680.2.3.300

Funder, D. C. (1995). On the accuracy of personality judgment: A realistic approach. *Psychological Review, 102*(4), 652. https://doi.org/10.1037/0033-295x.102.4.652

Funder, D. C. (1999). *Personality judgment: A realistic approach to person perception.* Academic Press.

Gawronski, B., & Bodenhausen, G. V. (2006). Associative and propositional processes in evaluation: An integrative review of implicit and explicit attitude change. *Psychological Bulletin, 132,* 692–731. https://doi.org/10.1037/0033-2909.132.5.692

Gawronski, B., & Bodenhausen, G. V. (2007). Unraveling the processes underlying evaluation: Attitudes from the perspective of the APE model. *Social Cognition, 25*, 687–717.

Gray, J. A. (1982). *The neuropsychology of anxiety: An enquiry into the functions of the septo-hippocampal system.* Clarendon Press.

Gray, J. A. (1987). The neuropsychology of emotion and personality. In S. M. Stahl, S. D. Iverson, & E. C. Goodman (Eds.), *Cognitive neurochemistry* (pp. 171–190). Oxford University Press.

Kock, N. (2005). Media richness or media naturalness? The evolution of our biological communication apparatus and its influence on our behavior toward E-communication tools. *IEEE Transactions on Professional Communication, 48*(2), 117–130. https://doi.org/10.1109/TPC.2005.849649

Kock, N. (2011). Media naturalness theory: Human evolution and behaviour towards electronic communication technologies. In S. C. Roberts (Ed.), *Applied evolutionary psychology* (pp. 380–398). Oxford University Press. https://doi.org/10.1093/acprof:oso/9780199586073.003.0023

Lakoff, G., & Johnson, M. (1980). *Metaphors we live by.* University of Chicago Press.

Nelson, D. L. (1979). Remembering pictures and words: Appearance, significance, and name. In L. S. Cermak & F. I. M. Craik (Eds.), *Levels of processing in human memory* (pp. 45–76). Erlbaum.

Paivio, A. (1971). *Imagery and verbal processes.* Holt, Rinehart and Winston.

Petty, R. E., & Cacioppo, J. T. (1986). The elaboration likelihood model of persuasion. *Advances in Experimental Social Psychology, 9*, 123–205. https://doi.org/10.1016/S0065-2601(08)60214-2

Snodgrass, J. G. (1980). Towards a model for picture and word processing. In P. A. Kolers, M. E. Wrolstad, & H. Bouma (Eds.), *Processing of visible language. Nato conference series* (Vol. 13). Springer. https://doi.org/10.1007/978-1-4684-1068-6_42

Van Kleef, G. A. (2009). How emotions regulate social life: The Emotions as Social Information (EASI) model. *Current Directions in Psychological Science, 18*(3), 184–188. https://doi.org/10.1111/j.1467-8721.2009.01633.x

Walther, J. B. (1992). Interpersonal effects in computer-mediated interaction. *Communication Research, 19*(1), 52–90. https://doi.org/10.1177/009365092019001003

Conceptual Approaches

Abstract Chapter 2 reviews the range of approaches that researchers have used to study how we process emoji. This includes: face processing, emotion recognition, psycholinguistics, grounded cognition and interpersonal processing. Chapter 2 provides an overview of the main principles of these approaches, the types of research questions these approaches have addressed and the relevant insights gained.

Keywords Emoji • Emotional • Face processing • Psycholinguistics • Emotion recognition • Interpersonal processing

This chapter provides a comprehensive review of the range of conceptual approaches that have been afforded to the study of emoji processing and what insights these have brought about. This provides an overview of the main principles of these approaches, the types of research questions these approaches have addressed and the relevant insights gained.

Within this chapter, you will see that conceptual approaches and principles in many cases are rather disparate from each other. The main reason for this is that the approach is largely motivated by the specific scholar's view about how emoji function within communication. That is, some scholars seek to understand the equivalence of emoji to faces in our

© The Author(s), under exclusive license to Springer Nature Switzerland AG 2024
L. K. Kaye, *The Psychology of Emoji Processing*, Palgrave Studies in Cyberpsychology,
https://doi.org/10.1007/978-3-031-75113-4_2

recognition and responses to emotion, some view emoji as serving complimentary non-verbal functions in written communication in a similar way to gestures within offline, "real world" communication while some seek to understand the lexical and/or semantic properties of emoji and their correspondence to linguistic components. Whilst these can each operate in parallel and need not be mutually exclusive, these have each drawn upon rather different approaches (yet wholly appropriate in each respective case) to understand how we process emoji.

In Chap. 1, Table 1.1 summarised the range of discipline approaches that have been afforded to the study of emoji processing which broadly sit under emotional processing, cognitive processing and interpersonal processing. This chapter will review these in turn and identify the respective insights and advancements these approaches may provide.

EMOTIONAL PROCESSING

Face Processing

A substantial strain of research on emoji has applied face-processing principles and asked associated research questions. This makes a lot of sense given that (facial) emoji are supposedly iconic of facial expressions. Broadly, scholars who approach the study of emoji from this perspective are interested in questions such as:

- To what extent do we use holistic or featural processing for emoji stimuli?
- How we process emotional expressions from emoji akin to faces?
- How does emotion recognition/categorisation ability compare between emoji and their face counterparts?
- Do we afford attentional vigilance to fearful or angry emoji in the same way as their face counterparts?

The field of face processing has a significant basis for the psychological study of emoji. Research within this field can help us understand a wide range of relevant issues such as the processes and correlates of emotional recognition (Kendall et al., 2016), how emotional expressions can guide our attention (Eastwood et al., 2001), how emotional expression supports facial recognition performance (D'Argembeau & Van der Linden, 2011; Tanaka et al., 2022), how we show a tendency to be vigilant to threatening faces such as anger (Calvo et al., 2006; Öhman et al., 2001), what features help us detect emotion (Calvo & Nummenmaa, 2008) and how different emotional expressions relate to recognition memory (Liu et al., 2014). Indeed, these are equally relevant areas of enquiry to apply to emoji, especially when ascertaining the extent to which emoji may operate in equivalent ways to faces within social information processing and/or communication.

Research which has compared faces and emoji has found that emoji increase the structural encoding process relative to faces (Gantiva et al., 2020), which has suggested that emoji are harder to process on a neurological level compared to human faces. Specifically, this is evidenced from emoji evoking lower N170 potentials and higher P3 amplitudes compared to human faces (Weiss et al., 2020). This suggests that they might not be the best to be considered as equivalent counterparts to faces with respect to how we encode them. Correspondingly, other neurological evidence suggests that emoji are less effective than facial expressions (Weiss et al., 2019). This assertion is also supported by research suggesting that emoji (relative to faces) appear to elicit more strongly in later-stage event-related brain potentials (e.g., evident in N2 responses) compared to earlier-stage ones where faces appear to elicit stronger responses (Liao et al., 2021). As such, this evidence seems to suggest that although emoji may draw upon similar neurological regions in the encoding of emoji (via categorisation, structural encoding etc), the degree of activation appears to be somewhat different between emoji and faces. From this, we might therefore be able to conclude that although processing of (facial) emoji may follow similar neurological mechanisms and serve similar functions as face counterparts with respect to helping us identify emotion, caution should be raised on the extent to which this is wholly equivalent in terms of the processing efficiency. This difference may, in part, be explained by the fact that unlike faces, recognising emotion from emoji does not hold the same immediate, "real-time" physical or social consequence. In the case of fear or anger being expressed for example, for faces, there is a significant "survival" advantage to be had from recognising these emotions, but in respect of emoji, because we are not typically physically co-located with the sender expressing these emotions, there is not the equivalent immediate physical or social threat.

Evidence from social neuroscience provides further insights into how we attend to visual information which might serve social benefit. This can be considered in respect of attentional bias in which we might tend to prioritise certain stimuli over others, particularly those which might be considered to be social threats (Eisenberger & Cole, 2012). Attentional bias can be assessed in many different ways, but one commonly used measure is the Dot Probe Task (discussed in further detail in Chap. 4). In theory, threatening stimuli (relative to neutral stimuli) should be being paid attention to, and as such, people are likely to respond much faster to stimuli which is subsequently occupying the same spatial location as a threatening stimuli than a neutral one. Indeed, it has been found that we have attentional bias towards stimuli which could be proposed to be threatening, such as angry faces (Cooper & Langton, 2006) or fearful faces (Bocanegra & Zeelenberg, 2011).

These principles are relevant to the study of emoji processing, as they might help elucidate whether the emotions depicted by emoji, such as anger or fear, are experienced in an equivalent way to their face counterparts. As such, this can go some way to explore whether the emotional expressions depicted on emoji serve the same purpose as facial expressions, and also whether we process these expressions as being representative of emotion concepts. However, our recent research has evidenced that this is not the case (MacKenzie et al., 2024). That is, we do not observe any difference in attentional vigilance towards negative emoji relative to neutral (or positive) ones, and this has been found to be the case both at early (100 ms) and later-stage (500 ms) stimuli onset. This is suggestive that we might not experience the emotions depicted on emoji in a way equivalent to their face counterparts.

Perhaps on a more basic level, we might want to understand whether the actual presentation of emotion on emoji corresponds anatomically to their facial expression counterparts. Interestingly, research which has used the "Facial Action Coding System (Ekman & Rosenberg, 1997) has found that as well as emoji appearance varying across platforms, most emoji faces do not adhere anatomically to expressions on human faces (Fugate & Franco, 2021).

The broader principle that we can take from this strain of research is the extent to which emoji are equivalent cues representing emotion or depicting emotional expression to that of faces within offline communication. The evidence, however, would suggest that this is not the case, largely due to the fact that we appear to process these less easily than faces, and might require later-stage or more executive levels of processing control relative to faces.

Emotion Recognition and Affective Dimensions

Another way scholars have approached the psychological study of emoji has been to understand the extent to which principles from emotion recognition can be applied to emoji. Whilst some of this research might sit within the face-processing field (e.g., if scholars are asking questions about what visual features might aid emotion recognition ability), there is a broader sub-discipline of affective science which is more exclusively set up to understand emotion recognition from a wider perspective.

This has generally been applied to answer questions such as:

- What are the neural correlates of emotion recognition of emoji (and are these equivalent to their face counterparts)?
- How are Unicode Emoji rated in terms of valence and arousal? (and other affective dimensions)?
- How does emoji valence impact on effectiveness and efficiency of processing?

Research which has explored the equivalence of emotional recognition/discrimination for emoji stimuli relative to facial expressions has typically used paradigms which manipulate the effects of congruent emoji to context conditions versus incongruent ones to test how emotional violations (expected from incongruence) can elicit neurological responses. Congruence is characterised by conditions or trials where the emotion depicted in the emoji is matched or expected with context information (e.g., a happy emoji presented with the word "happy"). Incongruence would be where they are mismatched.

For example, Yu et al. (2022) using event-related potentials (ERPs), explored the neurological features associated with emotional violations in emoji as well as faces and emotion words. As well as incongruent conditions eliciting longer response times, N400 effects were equivalently evident in response to emoji as they were in response to faces. Similarly, other research findings indicate that the neural responses to emoji are largely equivalent to those found in faces (Gantiva et al., 2020). Specifically, N170 amplitudes have been found to be especially prominent in response to emoji (Zhao et al., 2019), and the time-course for emoji processing is largely similar to that of face processing (Gantiva et al., 2020). Interestingly, other research has explored the perception of pain expressions and the extent to which this might be recognised equivalently from faces (Liao et al., 2021). Whilst at a behavioural level (measured via reaction times) pain appears to be recognised better from faces than emoji, the early-stage processing via P2 amplitudes and later-stage processing via LPP amplitudes suggest that pain is processed from emoji in a largely equivalent way to that expected from faces (ibid). Intriguingly, little research has corresponded to these insights towards the holistic versus featural processing of emoji to better understand how recognition/detection might be aligned to the way different facial features are discriminated. The use of eye-tracking methodology could present a helpful addition here to more fully explore how emotion detection might map to any bottom-up visual processing.

Taking a different approach, other research has sought to understand the affective dimensions afforded to emoji. This has typically taken the approach of explicit perception scales to measure endorsement or intensity ratings for different emoji stimuli, such as those on the Unicode list or Emojipedia. This seeks to establish how processing varies based on affective dimensions or characteristics which we afford to emoji. The wider field of emotion makes reference to the key dimensions valence and arousal (Bradley et al., 1992; Kuchinke et al., 2005). Valence relates to the pleasantness of the emotion (how positive or negative it is) and arousal to the intensity of the emotion (Feldman Barrett & Russell, 1998; Lang et al., 1997; Russell, 2003). In relation to emoji, these dimensions are equally relevant, in addition to other affective dimensions including familiarity, visual complexity/clarity, meaningfulness, concreteness and aesthetic appeal (Rodrigues et al., 2018). However, in respect of processing, previous research suggests that emoji may elicit lesser attentional orientation and engagement as well as lower arousal than face counterparts (Gantiva et al., 2020). Conversely, other research which has compared affective ratings of emoji and faces for dimensions of valence and arousal has found that emoji elicit higher ratings of arousal relative to faces, and that affective dimensions are recognised more effectively in emoji relative to faces (Fischer & Herbert, 2021). Whilst the direction of these various findings offers mixed perspectives, the fact that there are distinctions between emoji stimuli and faces suggests that they may not operate equivalently to face stimuli in respect of processing affective dimensions. Additionally, a key distinction is that structural features of emoji such as the number of visual features and visual complexity can vary quite extensively across emoji stimuli, as well as appear visually distinct across software/platforms (Miller et al., 2021). These distinctions have been found to affect the affective ratings that users afford to emoji (Miller et al., 2021; Rodrigues et al., 2018) and therefore mean that emoji lack universality in the affective judgements which are drawn from their processing.

Another approach to the study of affective judgements has involved exploring whether emoji impact the valence perceptions of accompanying (neutral) text (Hand et al., 2023; Neel et al., 2023). For example, Neel et al. (2023) found that messages which included negative emoji were consistently rated more negative and ones including positive emoji were consistently more positively rated, compared to when other emoji were used on the equivalent messages. However, diverse interpretations have been found to exist between different sub-samples of users (Hand et al., 2023). As such, whilst emoji appear to hold some weight in our (explicit) affective perceptions, these do not follow a uniform process, and therefore it is debatable on whether they hold a true, inherent affective conceptual role.

Affective Experiences

Another approach which has been applied to the psychological study of emoji is to explore how they might be (valid) indicators of affective experiences such as mood. This is distinct from the previous section, which outlined affective judgements (of stimuli), and instead relates to how representative emoji may be of current mood states. This is also somewhat distinct from other research which has focused on emotion. Whilst emotion and mood have been well established as being inter-related and fall under the same broader concept of affect, they are distinct constructs (Batson et al., 1992; Ketai, 1975). Whilst emotion is typically assumed to be a reaction to a given stimulus or event, mood is less specific and is instead said to be less intense and more enduring (Kumar, 1997).

To explore how emoji may be indicators of current or in-the-moment mood, this would require us to assess our current affective state and recognise the extent to which specific emoji may correspond accurately to reflect this state. This is distinct from emotion processing in that this typically would not consist of an introspective assessment of one's current affective state but instead would require a response (often categorical in nature) to a given emoji stimulus.

Our recent research has explored how emoji may be an efficient means by which to assess current mood (Kaye & Schweiger, 2023). Arguably, for more traditional scales or instruments which include words or statements, responses to these might be somewhat shaped by the lexicon afforded to describe these (Barrett, 2006), given that these labels might be involved in the retrieval of prior conceptual knowledge relating to the sensory or affective experiences associated with these (Gentner & Goldin-Meadows, 2003). A benefit of emoji is that they might alleviate this possibility and instead draw upon the more bottom-up processing of in-the-moment affective or sensory information from which to make a judgement about the current affective state.

To study this, we developed the Emoji PANAS, which is a modified version of the Positive and Negative Affect Schedule (Watson et al., 1988) but includes relevant emoji to represent the 20 mood adjectives of the scale (discussed in more detail in Chap. 4). We found that there was general consistency in people's responses to in-the-moment mood between the Emoji PANAS and standard PANAS at each given time point across several days. However, we also found that emoji might not always be valid indicators of mood when accounting for those with dominant personality traits relating to emotionality (emotional stability and extraversion). As such, although this proffers a novel approach to understand how we correspond affective experiences to emoji, there is more to establish on the diversities which might operate here between us.

Cognitive Processing

Psycholinguistics

Somewhat far removed from the research on face processing are other strains of research on emoji which have adopted principles from psycholinguistics. This strain generally seeks to understand how emoji function within the semantic binding, lexical processing or comprehension of accompanying text. However, there is also research which explores the phatic functions of emoji within written discourse (e.g., how emoji might be used for the purposes of social interaction). However, this tends to be explored from the perspective of the sender rather than from a receiver (e.g., how emoji might be used as a form of punctuation or "softener" to reduce abruptness or ambiguity in written discourse; Danesi, 2017). As such, I do not discuss this in detail within this section, and instead focus on the aforementioned themes of research on emoji within psycholinguistics. Here, emoji have generally been applied to answer questions such as:

- Do emoji support semantic processing of accompanying words?
- Are emoji processed like words?

Emoji research in psycholinguistics primarily focuses on semantic processing, comprehension and/or retrieval of semantic information from long-term memory. Research typically has focused on understanding the extent to which emoji might be processed like words, whether they are processed lexically akin to words, and their role in supporting semantic processing of written discourse (Barach et al., 2021; Paggio & Tse, 2022; Weissman et al., 2023, 2024). Evidence suggests that in cases where emoji are used congruently within written text (an emoji matches the concept that is represented in words), this might support more efficient semantic processing (Barach et al., 2021; Beyersmann et al., 2023). This might however be dependent upon the extent to which the emoji of interest have an adequate level of conventional lexicalised meaning for receivers (Weissman et al., 2023). Similarly, other research using eye gaze behaviour indicates that when emoji appear in sentence-final positions (relative to sentence-initial positions), this increases the duration of attention to sentences, suggesting emoji may be serving semantic binding or "wrap-up" functions (Robus et al., 2020). However, when emoji are used as replacement for words, this slows down the efficiency of processing, as evidenced by slower reading rates (Paggio & Tse, 2022).

Taken together, whilst emoji might not be fully semantically functional to replace words, it seems that they can support the effectiveness (but perhaps not the efficiency) of semantic processing of written language, when shared semantic concepts are represented. A note to raise however is that this might not be an equivalent effect between words which vary in concreteness. That is, in the case of emoji representing concepts which might be more concrete, the above principles appear to generally apply. However, when referring more specifically to how emoji may be used to represent emotion concepts (e.g, happiness) or represent valance within written discourse, the effects are less compelling. Specifically, matching the valence of emoji to words/sentences (e.g, using a positively-valenced emoji alongside a positively-valenced word) does not seem to aid categorisation of words or word processing efficiency, suggesting that when emoji are used in this way, this is not particularly helpful in supporting semantic

Table 2.1 Distinctions in semantic processing based on different types of word/sentence and emoji pairings

Type	Example	Supports semantic processing?
Valent congruent (Positive)	The team won the championship ☺	☒
Valent congruent (Negative)	The team was experiencing ill health ☹	☒
Concrete concept congruent	The team won the trophy 🏆	☑
Concrete concept replacement	The team won the 🏆	☒

processing of written language. Table 2.1 provides an illustrative summary of the distinctions in semantic processing based on different types of word/sentence and emoji pairings.

In respect of semantic processing and comprehension, as well as word concreteness being a potential reason for mixed findings, contradictions in the literature may also be attributable to the nature of measurement. That is, studies measuring implicit responses, such as via neurological components or eye-tracking, seem to elicit evidence of the facilitative effects of emoji, whilst behavioural measures present less consistent evidence. For example, research by Yang et al. (2020) found that at a neurological level, when using semantically congruent word and emoji pairings, emoji can serve as useful primes to reduce cognitive demands in semantic processing. However, on a behavioural level, emoji do not appear to hold any significant effects for linguistic processing/interpretation (Robus et al., 2020). A large majority of research adopting implicit measures has explored ERPs via neuroimaging methods to investigate how we semantically process emoji akin to their word counterparts (e.g., Weissman, 2019; Weissman et al., 2024). These have typically used paradigms which manipulate the semantic or lexical contingency in word and emoji pairings. Congruence is characterised by conditions or trials where the emotion or semantic meaning depicted in the emoji is matched or expected with accompanying word or sentence content (happy emoji with positively valenced content). Incongruence would be the converse.

ERP studies have found that varying the congruence of emoji and word pairings activates brain regions associated with language/text processing (Pfeifer et al., 2022), as well as emotional recognition of fear, disgust and anger (BA47) (Chatzichristos et al., 2020). Additionally, other research has found P200 and P600 effects in respect of verbal irony, which have been found to be equivalent for irony-producing emoji such as via the wink emoji (Weissman & Tanner, 2018). Further, equivalent N400 effects have been found for emoji, as might be expected for emotion words (Yu et al., 2022) and in respect of words (nouns) with equivalent lexical meaning (Weissman et al., 2024). For example, when comparing N400 effects in conditions where emoji represent either an expected versus unexpected semantic concept at the end of a sentence, N400 effects have been found to be elicited for unexpected emoji (Weisman et al., 2024). This suggests that lexical meaning from emoji is integrated in the processing of sentences.

However, not all research finds that emoji aid lexical processing or semantic retrieval. Namely, recent studies have explored ERP responses (N400 and P600) in conditions where emoji accompany semantically congruent versus incongruent sentences/words. Findings show that emoji compared to words elicit semantic retrieval hindrances (Tang et al., 2020) and appear neurologically more effortful to process (Tang et al., 2024), suggesting that semantic integration of emoji is not always akin to words (ibid).

Despite there being some evidence of facilitative effects for sematic processing at an implicit level, this is not always captured in cases where studies use behavioural measures. For example, our research, which explored the effects of congruence of emoji-word pairings (including instances where emoji are sequentially priming words), found no evidence of any effects on emotion categorisation of words or subsequent recall of words (Kaye et al., 2021, 2023). Conversely, other research using less "explicit" behavioural measures (namely, reaction times to key presses) has found significant effects in this regard. Namely, that emotionally congruent word and emoji pairings aid memory retrieval relating to the stimulus relative to incongruent pairings (Chatzichristos et al., 2020). As such, the literature presents somewhat disparate evidence about the role of emoji as semantic aids. However, this may be attributed to the nature of behavioural measures used across studies. That is, behavioural measures which are more implicit in nature (key presses) are perhaps somewhat different from those which are drawing more on explicit responses (recalling words), and thus may capture earlier-stage semantic retrieval processes.

To summarise, the mixed findings in this literature appear to be generally attributable to the type of concept emoji are being used to represent and perhaps more so, the nature of the experimental measurement. That is, whilst null findings appear quite commonplace in studies using behavioural tasks (e.g., reaction times, memory retrieval tasks), findings from studies that capture neurological processes (e.g., ERP components) or implicit measures (reading duration using eye gaze behaviour) seem to suggest, at least in some cases, that emoji (particularly those which represent concrete concepts) serve some role in semantic and/or linguistic processing.

Embodied/Grounded Cognition

There are various perspectives which are relevant to embodied cognition/ grounded cognition. Some of these relate to the metaphorical nature of our conceptual thought systems (Lakoff & Johnson, 1980), while others relate to the integration of sensorimotor or perceptual experiences into conceptual thought (Barsalou, 1999). These perspectives will be discussed in turn.

It has been argued that abstract cognition (which can apply to emotion concepts) can be based on physical metaphors (Lakoff & Johnson, 1980). More specifically, it is posited that our conceptual systems are metaphorical in nature and that metaphors influence our thinking and actions (Lakoff & Johnson, 1980). This might be a helpful conceptual basis to consider whether emoji might equally operate in a way expected of emotion concepts to gauge the extent to which they are actually embodied as emotion concepts in conceptual thought. This is discussed further in respect of Conceptual Metaphor Theory (Lakoff & Johnson, 1980) in Chap. 3.

Other perspectives posit that conceptual thought is a product of the way we integrate sensorimotor and perceptual experiences of concepts from our interaction with them in the physical world (Barsalou, 1999). Information we receive through our senses (i.e., sensorimotor information) is critical to the way we experience, navigate and make sense of the physical world. Scholars have argued that sensorimotor knowledge plays a fundamental role in conceptual thought (e.g., Connell et al., 2012; Connell & Lynott, 2012). When tackling questions about cognitive processing of visual stimuli such as emoji, we can draw on insights from this field regarding how the visuo-spatial or physical properties of stimuli play out in the efficiency and effectiveness of processing.

To understand how different concepts might have sensorimotor affordances, researchers have established sensory norms for concepts represented in stimuli such as words (Lynott et al., 2020). For example, the *Lancaster Sensorimotor Norms* established modality-specific norms for a set of 40,000 English words for each perceptual modality (haptic, olfactory, auditory, gustatory, visual) (Lynott et al., 2020). Findings show that perceptual strength (i.e., how strongly people rate the associated sensory response) can facilitate lexical categorisation of words, suggesting that sensorimotor affordances support the processing and/or integration of conceptual knowledge.

In respect of emoji stimuli, an equivalent approach could present a fruitful opportunity to advance our understanding of the sensorimotor affordances of emoji to help us better explore how concepts represented in emoji might correspond to conceptual knowledge processing and/or integration. Developing equivalent sensorimotor norms for emoji lists would help support ongoing research efforts to establish the extent to which emoji might be semantically-related to conceptual knowledge. Additionally, this could help us better recognise the richness of our experiences with emoji to add weight against the thesis that online communication is impoverish relative to offline counterparts.

In respect of more specifically testing the effects of visual or spatial features of stimuli on conceptual processing, typically research has considered physical features of stimuli such as size, shape, or colour (e.g., Palef & Olson, 1975). Additionally, the spatial properties of stimuli are routinely studied, based on where they are presented within the receiver's visual field (Zwaan & Yaxley, 2003). This has been tested using well-established behavioural tasks such as the Spatial Stroop task, discussed in more detail in Chap. 4. Broadly exploring the physical and spatial properties of stimuli can help establish the nature and extent to which our sensorimotor systems are involved in the way we process the (visual) world.

A large majority of research testing the effects of spatial properties of stimuli has used word stimuli (Mahon, 2015; Mahon & Caramazza, 2008; Thornton et al., 2013) and has tended to manipulate where they are presented across the vertical or horizontal axis. The relevance of the vertical axis (upper versus lower visual field) and horizontal axis (left versus right visual field) broadly is to assess spatial iconicity, that is, the extent to which there is correspondence between the symbolic features of the stimuli and its location. For example, on the vertical axis, when the word "attic" or "sky" are presented in the upper visual field, evidence suggests we are more efficient at responding to these compared to when they are presented in the lower visual field, and vice versa for words such as "basement" or "floor" (Šetić & Domijan, 2007; Zwaan & Yaxley, 2003). This is because the domain represented in the stimuli is embodied by links with concrete domains experienced in the physical world (e.g., the word "sky" in upper space). Embodiment here refers to the role of the body when processing information (Clark, 1998). As such, when these domains are presented in prototypical spatial locations where they would appear in the physical world, there is said to be a bodily/sensorimotor experience to aid conceptual processing (Lakoff & Johnson, 1980). As such, stimuli spatial features can be considered key factors in cognitive performance (Lu & Proctor, 1995).

However, whilst these principles might be more easily applied to stimuli which are symbol of concrete domains in the physical world (e.g., objects), there is further discussion about how this applies to the processing of emotion, and specifically, emoji as candidates within this line of enquiry. Here, we can be led by findings from Meier and Robinson (2004), who found associations between spatial location and emotion, whereby we tend to situate positive emotion in higher physical space ("I'm on a high") and negative emotion in lower space ("I'm feeling down"). Evidence of this effect has largely shown processing advantages (i.e., more efficient responses) when emotion words are paired in prototypical vertical space or physical bodily experiences (Dudscig et al., 2015; Fisher, 1964; Michalak et al., 2009).

So, applying this to emoji, if emoji are indeed valid candidates of emotion, then we should observe an equivalent effect based on their positioning on the vertical axis. That is, if a happy emoji is indeed symbolic of the emotion concept of happiness, then this should be easier for us to process when it is presented in prototypical (upper) vertical space. In summary, we would expect facilitative or interference effects here based on the contingency between emoji and its presentation in vertical space to help determine how emoji are integrated within our sensorimotor and/or affective knowledge systems.

Empirical research has started to test this for emoji (discussed below), as well as more specifically identifying whether spatial processing is associated with understanding the emoji itself (stimuli processing), evaluating the valence of the emoji (valence evaluation) or the outcome of the concept being activated (outcome of activation; Dudscig et al., 2015). Previous work on word processing has found the valence evaluation phase to be important when triggering effects which come from emotion–space interactions (de la Vega et al., 2012, 2013), and that it is valence evaluations which activate spatial metaphors rather than vice versa (Meier & Robinson, 2004).

Our research, as documented in Kaye et al. (2022, 2023) has studied spatial iconicity effects based on vertical positioning of emoji. In both cases, we used a modified spatial Stroop task (Emoji Spatial Stroop Task—discussed in Chap. 4) to assess whether positive and negative emoji presented in the upper visual field received different valence evaluations compared to when presented in central or lower visual field. Kaye et al. (2022) obtained explicit self-report valence evaluations per trial ("how positively and negatively do you perceive this emoji to be?") rated on a Likert scale, whereas Kaye et al. (2023) obtained implicit responses via measuring accuracy and latency of responding to "Is this happy?" or "Is this sad?" instructions on trials. Interestingly, we found divergent findings. When measured by explicit self-reports, we found evidence of spatial iconicity effects, specifically that positive emoji were evaluated to be significantly more positive when presented in upper vertical space compared to other conditions and negative emoji significantly more negative compared to other conditions. Conversely, in Kaye et al. (2023), we did not find any significant spatial iconicity effects when measuring implicit responding. Figure 2.1 provides a visual summary of these findings.

These findings together raise some intriguing insights about the processing of emoji. Our research using implicit response measures did not

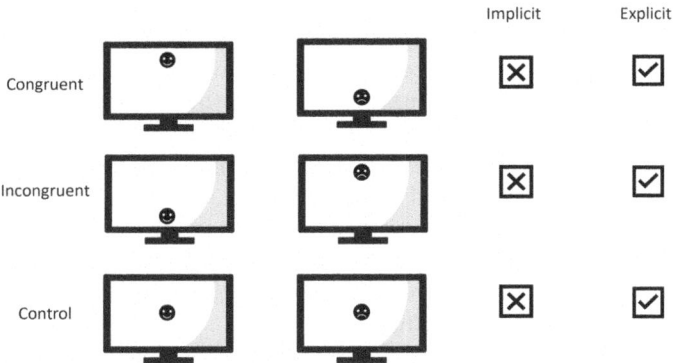

Fig. 2.1 Visual summary of effects of spatial iconicity on emoji processing

yield evidence to suggest that spatial properties impact emoji processing but our research using explicit response measures did. This may raise the assertion that emoji are processed at a later stage and thus any effects only become evidence when captured by measures which require a deliberative, conscious evaluation process, rather than a more automatic one (Kahneman, 2011). In the case of Kaye et al. (2023), this suggests there is not any activation of spatial metaphors within the valence evaluation process on an automatic, implicit level and instead, this might occur as a later-stage outcome following a more deliberative, valence evaluation process. To underpin this, we make specific reference to the theoretical framework of the Associative-Propositional Evaluation Model (Gawronski & Bodenhausen, 2006, 2007) to explain how such parallel processing models might be well placed to account for the automatic versus deliberate processing of emoji. This is discussed in further detail in Chap. 3.

To summarise, this section has applied the principles from cognitive science to refer to the role of visuo-spatial properties in the processing of stimuli. The evidence to date which has applied these principles is suggestive that emoji may not be encoded as emotion concepts but instead valence evaluations are activated based on deliberative, "slow" reasoning. This process might consist of the retrieval of conceptual knowledge which requires consideration of the contexts in which these types of emoji might typically be used, in order to aid categorisation/evaluation.

INTERPERSONAL PROCESSING

Research in this strand has approached the psychological study of emoji within the context of interpersonal interactions, and the extent to which they might impact upon perceptions of the message, the sender, or in some cases, attitudes/behaviours surrounding the message content. The main principles here are concerned with how emoji might function within interpersonal relationships and the impressions we make about others. Within this strand, theoretical frameworks are broadly drawn from the field of communication (or computer-mediated communication), such as Media Richness Theory (Daft & Lengel, 1986), social information processing or interpersonal perception theories within psychology. These are discussed in further detail in Chap. 3.

Among the research, scholars tend to take measures of receivers' perceptions. These have typically included message clarity (Hand et al., 2022), sender warmth (Boutet et al., 2021; Hand et al., 2022), sender responsiveness (Coyle & Carmichael, 2019), sender personality traits (Wall et al., 2016), relationship interest (Rodrigues et al., 2017), sender likeability (Riordan & Glikson, 2020), sender sincerity (Wang et al., 2023, 2023) and sender trustworthiness (Huang et al., 2021)

Research of this nature has typically manipulated the emotional congruence between messages and the accompanying emoji. Specifically, congruence between text and emoji has been found to be especially relevant to enhancing the emotional dimensions of the perceptions such as receivers' perceptions of message clarity and emotionality and sender warmth (Boutet et al., 2021; Hand et al., 2022). However, congruence is also important between the sender and receiver, as noted by Coyle and Carmichael (2019), who found that convergence in emoji use between interaction partners (both used emoji or neither used emoji) impacted upon receivers' perceptions of responsiveness, especially in the case of positive self-disclosures within messages.

In relation to interpersonal perceptions about the sender, research in this strain has explored how emoji use relates to trait judgements, particularly around personality characteristics. For example, evidence suggests that including positive emoticons/emoji in text can alleviate negative perceptions of others and feed into impressions about extraversion (Darbyshire et al., 2016; Fullwood & Martino, 2007). In respect of whether these are accurate judgements, evidence suggests that smiley emoji when used on Facebook feeds into accurate first impressions of others' extraversion and openness (Wall et al., 2016).

However, characteristics of the sender can also be a factor that impacts upon message perceptions, such as sender gender. That is, research has found that messages with affectionate emoji included are judged to be more appropriate and likeable when the sender is a woman compared to a man (Butterworth et al., 2019). However, this effect does not appear to be universal across all types of emoji, as this study also noted that perceptions of the message were judged equally when less affectionate emoji were used (ibid). Not only has sender gender been found to be impactful but also receiver gender appears to impact on perceptions afforded to messages with emoji (Riordan & Glikson, 2020). Specifically, male receivers are more likely to judge a sender to be more likeable and effective (in the context of leadership) than female receivers (ibid).

The principle about characteristics is important as it relates to a wider discussion about the role of individual differences in the processing and/ or interpretation of emoji. Whilst individual difference factors such as gender, age and culture might be considered to be relevant to other domains of emoji research, these factors tend to be most explicitly discussed within the interpersonal processing research or work which more generally falls under CMC. In relation to individual difference factors such as gender, this tends to be more relevant when asking questions such as "Do men or female tend to use more emoji?" which relates more to sender rather than receiver perspectives, so perhaps not so relevant to the scope of this book. However, the issue of age or generational effects of the interpretation of emoji remains a pertinent and highly sought-after query in public debate. Specifically, people query the extent to which there might be generational differences in emoji literacy and interpretation (George et al., 2023). Indeed, findings suggest that as well as cultural variations, there are nuanced emoji interpretations across ages of receivers, particularly when comparing those from Generation Z and Baby Boomers (Yue, 2022). Whilst it is likely that divergence in interpretation will be largely attributed to the type of emoji, with some prompting less consistent interpretations than others, this suggests that there are key sociocultural factors at play which should be recognised as relevant to the issue of emoji processing.

It is important to note that perceptions of messages and sender based on emoji use in messages are contextually bound. That is, studies have focused on how emoji might serve interpersonal perceptions within different types of relationships or levels of acquaintanceship such as romantic relationships (Rodrigues et al., 2017). Beyond this, whilst a significant proportion of research in this field has focused on what might be considered personal/social communication (e.g., close acquaintances, friends), other research has studied interpersonal perceptions associated with emoji within the context of e-commerce, such as brand-consumer communication (Cavalheiro et al., 2022; Prada et al., 2022; Wang et al., 2023a, b) and consumer reviews (Huang et al., 2021). Cavalheiro et al. (2022) found that perceptions of using emoji within brand-consumer interactions vary based on the platform of communication as well as age and frequency of emoji use of receivers. Within consumer complaint handling, evidence suggests that brands may wish to include emoji as this has been found to impact perceptions of sincerity which in turn leads to consumer forgiveness (Wang et al., 2023a, b). In respect of consumer reviews, evidence suggests that greater numbers of emoji used may be useful to signal review trustworthiness (Huang et al., 2021).

To summarise, the impacts of emoji on interpersonal perceptions are by no means universal. As with any type of behaviour, this occurs within a given context and interacts with a myriad of factors. As such, perceptions which are associated with the use of emoji vary based on factors including: convergence in emoji use between interaction partners (Coyle & Carmichael, 2019), gender of sender (Butterworth et al., 2019), gender of the receiver (Riordan & Glikson, 2020), context (personal, e-commerce, etc), platform of use (Cavalheiro et al., 2022), age of receiver (Cavalheiro et al., 2022) and frequency of receiver emoji use (Cavalheiro et al., 2022).

As such, it does not seem possible to draw conclusions about the nature of perceptions which receivers infer from emoji use, and therefore questions whether it is appropriate to assume universality of this. That is, the diversity of contexts, characteristics of sender/receivers and purposes of messages means that the interpersonal function of emoji will be equally diverse in respect of its impact on perception formation.

SUMMARY

Within this chapter, I have reviewed the various conceptual approaches and principles which have been applied to the study of emoji. As I am sure you can appreciate, many of these are somewhat disparate in nature and so drawing together any sort of consensus or take-home summaries from this is challenging. However, a general theme which I feel is consistent is the notion that there are no universal processing "laws" which appear to exist on how we process emoji. That is, diversity in processing seems to exist and can be attributed to many different factors, including what type of emotion is being depicted on emoji, emoji presentation (e.g., what platform/software, which specific UniCode emoji, visual complexity, etc), the context they are being used in, who the sender is, and how researchers are measuring the specific type of processing/interpretation.

The following chapters will review in more specific detail the theoretical frameworks which have been typically applied to these conceptual areas (Chap. 3) and the methodological paradigms which have been used to measure emoji processing (Chap. 4).

References

Barach, E., Feldman, L. B., & Sheridan, H. (2021). Are emojis processed like words?: Eye movements reveal the time course of semantic processing for emojified text. *Psychonomic Bulletin Review, 28,* 978–991. https://doi.org/10.3758/s13423-020-01864-y

Barrett, L. F. (2006). Are emotions natural kinds? *Perspectives on Psychological Science, 1*(1), 28–58. https://doi.org/10.1111/j.1745-6916.2006.00003.x

Barsalou, L. W. (1999). Perceptual symbol systems. *Behavioral and Brain Sciences, 22,* 577–660. https://doi.org/10.1017/s0140525x99002149

Batson, C. D., Shaw, L. L., & Oleson, K. C. (1992). Differentiating affect, mood, and emotion: Toward functionally based conceptual distinctions. In M. S. Clark (Ed.), *Emotion* (pp. 294–326). Sage Publications.

Beyersmann, E., Wegener, S., & Kemp, N. (2023). That's good news ☺: Semantic congruency effects in emoji processing. *Journal of Media Psychology: Theories, Methods, and Applications, 35*(1), 17–27. https://doi.org/10.1027/1864-1105/a000342

Bocanegra, B. R., & Zeelenberg, R. (2011). Emotional cues enhance the attentional effects on spatial and temporal resolution. *Psychonomic Bulletin & Review, 18*(6), 1071–1076. https://doi.org/10.3758/s13423-011-0156-

Boutet, I., LeBlanc, M., Chamberland, J. A., & Collin, C. A. (2021). Emojis influence emotional communication, social attributions, and information processing. *Computers in Human Behavior, 119,* 106722. https://doi.org/10.1016/j.chb.2021.106722

Bradley, M. M., Greenwald, M. K., Petry, M. C., & Lang, P. J. (1992). Remembering pictures: Pleasure and arousal in memory. *Journal of Experimental Psychology. Learning, Memory, and Cognition, 18*(2), 379–390. https://doi.org/10.1037/0278-7393.18.2.379

Butterworth, S. E., Giuliano, T. A., White, J., Cantu, L., & Fraser, K. C. (2019). Sender gender influences emoji interpretation in text messages. *Frontiers in Psychology, 10.* https://doi.org/10.3389/fpsyg.2019.00784

Calvo, M., Avero, P., & Lundqvist, D. (2006). Facilitated detection of angry faces: Initial orienting and processing efficiency. *Cognition and Emotion, 20*(6), 785–811. https://doi.org/10.1080/02699930500465224

Calvo, M. G., & Nummenmaa, L. (2008). Detection of emotional faces: Salient physical features guide effective visual search. *Journal of Experimental Psychology: General, 137*(3), 471–494. https://doi.org/10.1037/a0012771

Cavalheiro, B. P., Prada, M., Rodrigues, D. L., Garrido, M. V., & Lopes, D. (2022). With or without Emoji? Perceptions about emoji use in different brand-consumer communication contexts. *Human Behavior and Emerging Technologies, 2022,* 3036664. https://doi.org/10.1155/2022/3036664

Chatzichristos, C., Morante, M., Andreadis, N., Kofidis, E., Kopsinis, Y., & Theodoridis, S. (2020). Emojis influence autobiographical memory retrieval from reading words: An fMRI-based study. *PLoS One, 15*(7), e0234104. https://doi.org/10.1371/journal.pone.0234104

Clark, A. (1998). *Being there: Putting brain, body, and world together again.* MIT Press.

Connell, L., & Lynott, D. (2012). Strength of perceptual experience predicts word processing performance better than concreteness or imageability. *Cognition, 125*(3), 452–465. https://doi.org/10.1016/j.cognition.2012.07.010

Connell, L., Lynott, D., & Dreyer, F. (2012). A functional role for modality-specific perceptual systems in conceptual representations. *PLoS One, 7*(3), e33321. https://doi.org/10.1371/journal.pone.0033321

Cooper, R. M., & Langton, S. R. (2006). Attentional bias to angry faces using the Dot Probe task? It depends when you look for it. *Behaviour Research and Therapy, 44*(9), 1321–1329. https://doi.org/10.1016/j.brat.2005.10.004

Coyle, M. A., & Carmichael, C. L. (2019). Perceived responsiveness in text messaging: The role of emoji use. *Computers in Human Behavior, 99*, 181–189. https://doi.org/10.1016/j.chb.2019.05.023

D'Argembeau, A., & Van der Linden, M. (2011). Influence of facial expressions on memory for facial identity: Effects of visual features on emotional meaning. *Emotion, 11*(1), 199–202. https://doi.org/10.1037/a0022592

Daft, R. L., & Lengel, R. H. (1986). Organizational information requirements, media richness and structural design. *Management Science, 32*(5), 554–571. https://doi.org/10.1287/mnsc.32.5.554

Danesi, M. (2017). *The semiotics of emoji: The rise of visual language in the age of the internet.* Bloomsbury Publishing.

Darbyshire, D. E., Kirk, C., Wall, H. J., & Kaye, L. K. (2016). Don't judge a (Face)Book by its cover: Exploring judgement accuracy of others' personality on Facebook. *Computers in Human Behavior, 58*, 380–387. https://doi.org/10.1016/j.chb.2016.01.021

de la Vega, I., de Filippis, M., Lachmair, M., Dudschig, C., & Kaup, B. (2012). Emotional valence and physical space: Limits of interaction. *Journal of Experimental Psychology: Human Perception and Performance, 38*(2), 375–385. https://doi.org/10.1037/a0024979

de la Vega, I., Dudschig, C., De Filippis, M., Lachmair, M., & Kaup, B. (2013). Keep your hands crossed: The valence-by-left/right interaction is related to hand, not side, in an incongruent hand–response key assignment. *Acta Psychologica, 142*(2), 273–277. https://doi.org/10.1016/j.actpsy.2012.12.011

Dudscig, C., de la Vega, I., & Kaup, B. (2015). What's up? Emotion-specific activation of vertical space during language processing. *Acta Psychologica, 156,* 143–155. https://doi.org/10.1016/j.actpsy.2014.09.015

Eastwood, J. D., Smilek, D., & Merikle, P. M. (2001). Differential attentional guidance by unattended faces expressing positive and negative emotion. *Perception & Psychophysics, 63*(6), 1004–1013. https://doi.org/10.3758/bf03194519

Eisenberger, N. I., & Cole, S. W. (2012). Social neuroscience and health: Neurophysiological mechanisms linking social ties with physical health. *Nature Neuroscience, 15*(5), 669–674. https://doi.org/10.1038/nn.3086

Ekman, P., & Rosenberg, E. (1997). *What the face reveals: Basic and applied studies of spontaneous expression using the facial action coding system (FACS).* Oxford University Press.

Feldman Barrett, L., & Russell, J. A. (1998). The structure of current affect: Controversies and emerging consensus. *Current Directions in Psychological Science, 8,* 10–14.

Fischer, B., & Herbert, C. (2021). Emoji as affective symbols: Affective judgments of emoji, emoticons, and human faces varying in emotional content. *Frontiers in Psychology, 12.* https://doi.org/10.3389/fpsyg.2021.645173

Fisher, S. (1964). Depressive affect and perception of up-down. *Journal of Psychiatric Research, 2,* 25–30. https://doi.org/10.1176/appi.psychotherapy.1965.19.1.172

Fugate, J. M. B., & Franco, C. L. (2021). Implications for emotion: Using anatomically based facial coding to compare emoji faces across platforms. *Frontiers in Psychology, 12.* https://doi.org/10.3389/fpsyg.2021.605928

Fullwood, C., & Martino, O. I. (2007). Emoticons and impression formation. *Applied Semiotics, 19*(8), 4–14.

Gantiva, C., Sotaquirá, M., Araujo, A., & Cuervo, P. (2020). Cortical processing of human and emoji faces: An ERP analysis. *Behaviour & Information Technology,39*(8),935–943.https://doi.org/10.1080/0144929X.2019.1632933-

Gawronski, B., & Bodenhausen, G. V. (2006). Associative and propositional processes in evaluation: An integrative review of implicit and explicit attitude change. *Psychological Bulletin, 132,* 692–731. https://doi.org/10.1037/0033-2909.132.5.692

Gawronski, B., & Bodenhausen, G. V. (2007). Unraveling the processes underlying evaluation: Attitudes from the perspective of the APE model. *Social Cognition, 25,* 687–717.

Gentner, D., & Goldin-Meadows, S. (Eds.). (2003). *Language in mind.* MIT Press.

George, A. S., Hovan George, A. S., & Baskar, T. (2023). Emoji unite: Examining the rise of emoji as an international language bridging cultural and generational divides. *Partners Universal International Innovation Journal, 1*(4), 183–204. https://doi.org/10.5281/zenodo.8280356

Hand, C. J., Burd, K., Oliver, A., & Robus, C. M. (2022). Interactions between text content and emoji types determine perceptions of both messages and senders. *Computers in Human Behavior Reports, 8*, 100242. https://doi.org/10.1016/j.chbr.2022.100242

Hand, C. J., Kennedy, A., Filik, R., Pitchford, M., & Robus, C. M. (2023). Emoji identification and emoji effects on sentence emotionality in ASD-diagnosed adults and neurotypical controls. *Journal of Autism and Developmental Disorders, 53*(6), 2514–2528. https://doi.org/10.1007/s10803-022-05557-4)

Huang, Y., Ma, J., Wu, C.-H., & Yang, S. (2021). An emoji is worth a thousand words? The influence of face emojis on consumer perceptions of user-generated reviews. *Journal of Global Information Management, 29*(6). https://doi.org/10.4018/JGIM.20211101.oa2

Kahneman, D. (2011). *Thinking, fast and slow.* Farrar, Straus and Giroux.

Kaye, L. K., Darker, G., Rodriguez Cuadrado, S., Wall, H. J., & Malone, S. A. (2022). The Emoji Spatial Stroop task: Exploring the impact of vertical positioning of emoji on emotional processing. *Computers in Human Behavior*, 107267. https://doi.org/10.1016/j.chb.2022.107267

Kaye, L. K., MacKenzie, A. K., Rodriguez-Cuadrado, S., Malone, S. A., Stacey, J., & Garrot, E. (2023). (Not) Feeling up or down?: Lack of evidence for vertical spatial iconicity effects for valence evaluations of emoji stimuli. *Computers in Human Behavior, 149*, 107931. https://doi.org/10.1016/j.chb.2023.107931

Kaye, L. K., Rocabado, J. F., Rodriguez Cuadrado, S., Jones, B. R., Malone, S. A., Wall, H. J., & Duñabeitia, J. A. (2023). Exploring the (lack of) facilitative effect of emoji for emotional word processing. *Computers in Human Behavior, 139*, 107563. https://doi.org/10.1016/j.chb.2022.107563

Kaye, L. K., Rodriguez Cuadrado, S., Malone, S. A., Wall, H. J., Gaunt, E., Mulvey, A. L., & Graham, C. (2021). How emotional are emoji?: Exploring the effect of emotional valence on the processing of emoji stimuli. *Computers in Human Behavior, 116*, 106648.

Kaye, L. K., & Schweiger, C. R. (2023). Are emoji valid indicators of in-the-moment mood? *Computers in Human Behavior, 148*, 107916. https://doi.org/10.1016/j.chb.2023.107916

Kendall, L. N., Raffaelli, Q., Kingstone, A., & Todd, R. M. (2016). Iconic faces are not real faces: Enhanced emotion detection and altered neural processing as faces become more iconic. *Cognitive Research: Principles and Implications, 1*(19). https://doi.org/10.1186/s41235-016-0021-8

Ketai, R. (1975). Affect, mood, emotion, and feeling: Semantic considerations. *The American Journal of Psychiatry, 132*(11), 1215–1217. https://doi.org/10.1176/ajp.132.11.1215

Kuchinke, L., Jacobs, A. M., Grubich, C., Vo, M. L.-H., Conrad, M., & Hermann, M. (2005). Incidental effects of emotional valence in single word processing: An fMRI study. *NeuroImage, 28*(4), 1022–1032. https://doi.org/10.1016/j.neuroimage.2005.06.050

Kumar, R. (1997). The role of affect in negotiations: An integrative overview. *The Journal of Applied Behavioral Science, 33*, 84–100. https://doi.org/10.1177/0021886397331007

Lakoff, G., & Johnson, M. (1980). *Metaphors we live by.* University of Chicago Press.

Lang, P. J., Bradley, M. M., & Cuthbert, B. N. (1997). Motivated attention: Affect, activation, and action. In P. J. Lang, R. F. Simons, & M. T. Balaban (Eds.), *Attention and orienting: Sensory and motivational processes* (pp. 97–135). Erlbaum.

Liao, W., Zhang, Y., Huang, X., Xu, X., & Peng, X. (2021). "Emoji, I can feel your pain" – Neural responses to facial and emoji expressions of pain. *Biological Psychology, 163*, 108134. https://doi.org/10.1016/j.biopsycho.2021.108134

Liu, C. H., Chen, W., & Ward, J. (2014). Remembering faces with emotional expressions. *Frontiers in Psychology, 5*, Article 1439. https://doi.org/10.3389/psyg.2014.01439

Lu, C. H., & Proctor, R. W. (1995). The influence of irrelevant location information on performance: A review of the Simon and spatial Stroop effects. *Psychonomic Bulletin & Review, 2*(2), 174–207. https://doi.org/10.3758/BF03210959

Lynott, D., Connell, L., Brysbaert, M., Brand, J., & Carney, J. (2020). The Lancaster Sensorimotor Norms: Multidimensional measures of perceptual and action strength for 40,000 English words. *Behavior Research Methods, 52*, 1271–1291. https://doi.org/10.3758/s13428-019-01316-z

MacKenzie, A. K., Stacey, J. E., Rodriguez-Cuadrado, S., Malone, S. A., Pimprikar, A., & Kaye, L. K. (2024, July 1). *Emoji are not emotional: Evidence from an attention probe task.* [Oral presentation] British Psychological Society's Cyberpsychology Section Annual Conference.

Mahon, B. Z. (2015). The burden of embodied cognition. *Canadian Journal of Experimental Psychology, 69*, 172–178. https://doi.org/10.1037/cep0000060

Mahon, B. Z., & Caramazza, A. (2008). A critical look at the embodied cognition hypothesis and a new proposal for grounding conceptual content. *Journal of Physiology, Paris, 102*, 59–70. https://doi.org/10.1016/j.jphysparis.2008.03.004

Meier, B. P., & Robinson, M. D. (2004). Why the sunny side is up: Associations between affect and vertical position. *Psychological Science, 15*(4), 243–247. https://doi.org/10.1111/j.0956-7976.2004.00659.x

Michalak, J., Troje, N. F., Fischer, J., Vollmar, P., Heidenreich, T., & Schulte, D. (2009). Embodiment of sadness and depression—Gait patterns associated with dysphoric mood. *Psychosomatic Medicine, 71*(5), 580–587. https://doi.org/10.1097/PSY.0b013e3181a2515c

Miller, H., Thebault-Spieker, J., Chang, S., Johnson, I., Terveen, L., & Hecht, B. (2021). "Blissfully Happy" or "Ready to Fight": Varying interpretations of emoji. *Proceedings of the International AAAI Conference on Web and Social Media, 10*(1), 259–268. https://doi.org/10.1609/icwsm.v10i1.14757

Neel, L. A. G., McKechnie, J. G., Robus, C. M., & Hand, C. J. (2023). Emoji alter the perception of emotion in affectively neutral text messages. *Journal of Nonverbal Behavior, 47,* 83–97. https://doi.org/10.1007/s10919-022-00421-6

Öhman, A., Lundqvist, D., & Esteves, F. (2001). The face in the crowd revisited: A threat advantage with schematic stimuli. *Journal of Personality and Social Psychology, 80*(3), 381–396. https://doi.org/10.1037/0022-3514.80.3.381

Paggio, P., & Tse, A. P. P. (2022). Are emoji processed like words? An eye-tracking study. *Cognitive Science, 46,* e13099. https://doi.org/10.1111/cogs.13099

Palef, S. R., & Olson, D. R. (1975). Spatial and verbal rivalry in a Stroop-like task. *Canadian Journal of Psychology, 29*(3), 201–209. https://doi.org/10.1037/h0082026

Pfeifer, V. A., Armstrong, E. L., & Lai, V. T. (2022). Do all facial emojis communicate emotion? The impact of facial emojis on perceived sender emotion and text processing. *Computers in Human Behavior, 126,* 107016. https://doi.org/10.1016/j.chb.2021.107016

Prada, M., Saraiva, M., Cruz, S., Xavier, S., & Rodrigues, D. L. (2022). Using emoji in response to customer reservation requests and service reviews. *Human Behavior and Emerging Technologies, 2022,* 1433055. https://doi.org/10.1155/2022/1433055

Riordan, M. A., & Glikson, E. (2020). On the hazards of the technology age: How using emojis affects perceptions of leaders. *International Journal of Business Communication.* https://doi.org/10.1177/2329488420971690

Robus, C. M., Hand, C. J., Filik, R., & Pitchford, M. (2020). Investigating effects of emoji on neutral narrative text: Evidence from eye movements and perceived emotional valence. *Computers in Human Behavior, 109,* 106361. https://doi.org/10.1016/j.chb.2020.106361

Rodrigues, D., Lopes, D., Prada, M., Thompson, D., & Garrido, M. V. (2017). A frown emoji can be worth a thousand words: Perceptions of emoji use in text messages exchanged between romantic partners. *Telematics and Informatics, 34*(8), 1532–1543. https://doi.org/10.1016/j.tele.2017.07.001

Rodrigues, D., Prada, M., Gaspar, R., Garrido, M. V., & Lopes, D. (2018). Lisbon Emoji and Emoticon Database (LEED): Norms for emoji and emoticons in seven evaluative dimensions. *Behavior Research Methods, 50*(1), 392–405. https://doi.org/10.3758/s13428-017-0878-6

Russell, J. A. (2003). Core affect and the psychological construction of emotion. *Psychological Review, 110*(1), 145–172.

Šetić, M., & Domijan, D. (2007). The influence of vertical spatial orientation on property verification. *Language & Cognitive Processes, 22*, 297–312. https://doi.org/10.1080/01690960600732430

Tanaka, Y., Ishikawa, K., Oyama, T., & Okubo, M. (2022). Face inversion does not affect the reversed congruency effect of gaze. *Psychonomic Bulletin and Review.* https://doi.org/10.3758/s13423-022-02208-8

Tang, M., Chen, B., Zhao, X., & Zhao, L. (2020). Processing network emojis in Chinese sentence context: An ERP study. *Neuroscience Letters, 722*, 134815. https://doi.org/10.1016/j.neulet.2020.134815

Tang, M., Chen, B., Zhao, X., & Zhao, L. (2024). Semantic and syntactic processing of emojis in sentential intermediate positions. *Cognitive Neurodynamics, 18*, 1743–1752. https://doi.org/10.1007/s11571-023-10037-1

Thornton, T., Loetscher, T., Yates, M. J., & Nicholls, M. E. R. (2013). The highs and lows of the interaction between word meaning and space. *Journal of Experimental Psychology, 39*, 964–973. https://doi.org/10.1037/a0030467

Wall, H. J., Taylor, P. J., & Campbell, C. (2016). Getting the balance right? A mismatch in interaction demands between target and judge impacts on judgement ac curacy for some traits but not others. *Personality and Individual Differences, 88*, 66–72. https://doi.org/10.1016/j.paid.2015.08.037

Wang, X., Cheng, M., Zhu, J., & Jiang, R. (2023a). When texts meet emoji: A multi-stage study of tourism brands. *Journal of Travel Research.* https://doi.org/10.1177/00472875231203396

Wang, K.-Y., Chih, W.-H., & Honora, A. (2023b). How the emoji use in apology messages influences customers' responses in online service recoveries: The moderating role of communication style. *International Journal of Information Management, 69*, 102618. https://doi.org/10.1016/j.ijinfomgt.2022.102618

Watson, D., Clark, L. A., & Tellegen, A. (1988). Development and validation of brief measures of positive and negative affect: The PANAS scales. *Journal of Personality and Social Psychology, 54*, 1063–1070. https://doi.org/10.1037/0022-3514.54.6.1063

Weiss, M., Gutzeit, J., Rodrigues, J., Mussel, P., & Hewig, J. (2019). Do emojis influence social interactions? Neural and behavioral responses to affective emojis in bargaining situations. *Psychophysiology, 56*(4), e13321. https://doi.org/10.1111/psyp.13321

Weiss, M., Mussel, P., & Hewig, J. (2020). The value of a real face: Differences between affective faces and emojis in neural processing and their social influence on decision-making. *Social Neuroscience, 15*(3), 255–268. https://doi.org/10.1080/17470919.2019.1675758

Weissman, B. (2019). Emojis in sentence processing: An electrophysiological approach. In *Companion proceedings of the 2019 world wide web conference (WWW '19)* (pp. 478–479). Association for Computing Machinery. https://doi.org/10.1145/3308560.3316544

Weissman, B., Cohn, N., & Tanner, D. (2024). The electrophysiology of lexical prediction of emoji and text. *Neuropsychologia, 198*, 108881. https://doi.org/10.1016/j.neuropsychologia.2024.108881

Weissman, B., Engelen, J., Bass, E., & Cohn, N. (2023). The Lexicon of emoji? Conventionality modulates processing of emoji. *Cognitive Science, 47*(4), e13275. https://doi.org/10.1111/cogs.13275

Weissman, B., & Tanner, D. (2018). A strong wink between verbal and emoji-based irony: How the brain processes ironic emojis during language comprehension. *PLoS One, 13*(8), e0201727. https://doi.org/10.1371/journal.pone.0201727

Yang, J., Yang, Y., Xiu, L., & Yu, G. (2020). Effect of emoji prime on the understanding of emotional words – Evidence from ERPs. *Behaviour & Information Technology, 41*(6), 1313–1322. https://doi.org/10.1080/0144929X.2021.1874050

Yu, L., Xu, Q., Cao, F., Liu, J., Zheng, J., Yang, Y., & Zhang, L. (2022). Emotional violation of faces, emojis, and words: Evidence from N400. *Biological Psychology, 173*, 108405. https://doi.org/10.1016/j.biopsycho.2022.108405

Yue, L. (2022). *"Do you know what I mean?" An intercultural cross-generational study on emoji interpretation.* Doctoral dissertation, Radboud University. https://theses.ubn.ru.nl/items/8a2b2241-9e19-472b-9b31-bcec20415ca3

Zhao, J., Meng, Q., An, L., & Wang, Y. (2019). An event-related potential comparison of facial expression processing between cartoon and real faces. *PLoS One, 14*, e0198868. https://doi.org/10.1371/journal.pone.019886

Zwaan, R. A., & Yaxley, R. H. (2003). Spatial iconicity affects semantic relatedness judgments. *Psychonomic Bulletin & Review, 10*(4), 954–958. https://doi.org/10.3758/BF03196557

CHAPTER 3

Theoretical Frameworks

Abstract Chapter 3 reviews a range of specific theoretical frameworks that are suited to explore key mechanisms of emoji processing. This is distinctive from Chap. 2 in respect of identifying specific theories rather than broader approaches. This helps better explain how the features of these theoretical frameworks might be operationalised within research to address certain research questions and used within certain paradigms. Theories are situated under broader approaches of emotional processing, cognitive processing and interpersonal processing. Examples of theoretical frameworks include: The Associative-Propositional Evaluation Model (Gawronski & Bodenhausen, *Psychological Bulletin 132*:692–731, 2006; *Social Cognition 25*:687–717, 2007), Broaden-and-Build theory (Fredrickson, *Review of General Psychology 2*:300–319, 1998), Reinforcement sensitivity theory (RST; Gray, *The neuropsychology of anxiety: An enquiry into the functions of the septo-hippocampal system.* Clarendon Press, 1982; *Cognitive neurochemistry*:171–190. Oxford University Press, 1987), Conceptual Metaphor Theory (Lakoff & Johnson, *Metaphors we live by.* University of Chicago Press, 1980), Perceptual symbol systems framework (Barsalou, *Behavioral and Brain Sciences 22*:577–660, 1999), Sensory-semantic model (Nelson, *Levels of processing in human memory*:45–76. Erlbaum, 1979), Dual Coding Model (Paivio, *Imagery and verbal processes.* Holt, Rinehart and Winston, 1971), Prototypical Model of Picture and Word Processing (Snodgrass, *Processing of visible language. Nato conference series*, Vol. 13.

L. K. Kaye, *The Psychology of Emoji Processing*, Palgrave Studies in Cyberpsychology,
https://doi.org/10.1007/978-3-031-75113-4_3

Springer, 1980), Social Information Processing Theory (Walther, *Communication Research 19*:52–90, 1992), Emotion As Social Information Model (EASI; Van Kleef, *Current Directions in Psychological Science 18*:184–188, 2009), Media Richness Theory (Daft & Lengel, *Management Science 32*:554–571, 1986), Media Naturalness Theory (Kock, *IEEE Transactions on Professional Communication 48*:117–130, 2005; *Applied evolutionary psychology*:380–398. Oxford University Press, 2011), Channel Expansion Theory (Carlson & Zmud, *Academy of Management Journal 42*:153–170, 1999), Elaboration Likelihood Model (Petty & Cacioppo, 1986) and the Realistic Accuracy Model (Funder, *Psychological Review 102*:652, 1995). Chapter 3 includes a summary of key take-away points which synthesise which theoretical framework might be best suited to understanding different types of questions about how we process emoji.

Keywords Emoji • Emotional processing • Cognitive processing • Interpersonal processing • Emoji valence • Semantic processing • Theory

This chapter focuses more specifically on the value of specific theoretical frameworks that might be best suited to understand key mechanisms in the processing of emoji. This is distinctive from Chap. 2 in that I outline specific theories rather than broader approaches. This helps better explain how the features of these theoretical frameworks might be operationalised in research to address certain research questions and used in certain paradigms. This can help scholars in this field establish stronger theoretical underpinning for developing research questions, aligned to specific discipline traditions and paradigms. Discussion of these theoretical frameworks is situated under broad headings of how these correspond to conceptual ideas about emoji.

EMOTIONAL FUNCTIONS OF EMOJI

The Associative-Propositional Evaluation Model (Gawronski & Bodenhausen, 2006, 2007)

The basic operating principle of the Associative-Propositional Evaluation model (Gawronski & Bodenhausen, 2006, 2007) is that associative linking is the creation of a new association between two concepts based on their co-occurrence (Gawronski & Bodenhausen, 2009). In respect of emoji and emotion-laden words, associations between these can arguably be strengthened by the fact that these typically co-exist based on contingency with a shared valence concept (e.g., a positive emoji may tend to co-occur with words depicting positive sentiment). As such, words and emoji which are proposed to share equivalent valence properties may hold strong associative links. Conversely, an emoji with valence which is incongruent with the valence represented in a co-occurring word would be said to lack an associative link to a shared emotional concept.

The Associative-Propositional Evaluation model draws distinction between these basic operating principles of the associative process, and the secondary conditions of its operation (Gawronski & Bodenhausen, 2009, 2011). Specifically, for associative linking (which is arguably implicit in nature), the evaluation or outcome of this process can equally be automatic or controlled. In the case of automatic evaluation (e.g., via implicit response measures such as lexical decision tasks), this is void of any implied validity of a mental association between concepts. That is, the link may exist but without subjective judgement about whether this is valid. However, for controlled evaluation (such as via explicit rating or subjective reporting), this reflects the validity of this association as the individual engages in propositional processes to act upon this (Gawronski & Bodenhausen, 2011). See Fig. 3.1 for an example of how the Associative-Propositional Evaluation model might apply to emoji processing.

This theory can be especially useful for researchers who may be asking questions about the implicit vs explicit nature of how we form valence judgements of emoji or establishing whether there are conceptual emotional violations between emoji stimuli and their word or face counterparts. Explicit responses might include self-report perception ratings of stimuli, and implicit responses might be measured via EEG, fMRI or behavioural tasks such as lexical decision or Stroop tasks (discussed in Chap. 4).

Broaden-and-Build Theory (Fredrickson, 1998)

Broaden-and-Build theory (Fredrickson, 1998) is situated within the field of Positive Psychology and posits that certain discrete emotions can enhance people's in-moment thought-action processes. This is said to work in distinct ways for positive and negative emotions. Negative emotions narrow the thought-action repertoire, and can therefore be a short-circuit to behavioural responding (Fredrickson, 2001). However, positive emotions are said to extend people's modes of thinking and acting,

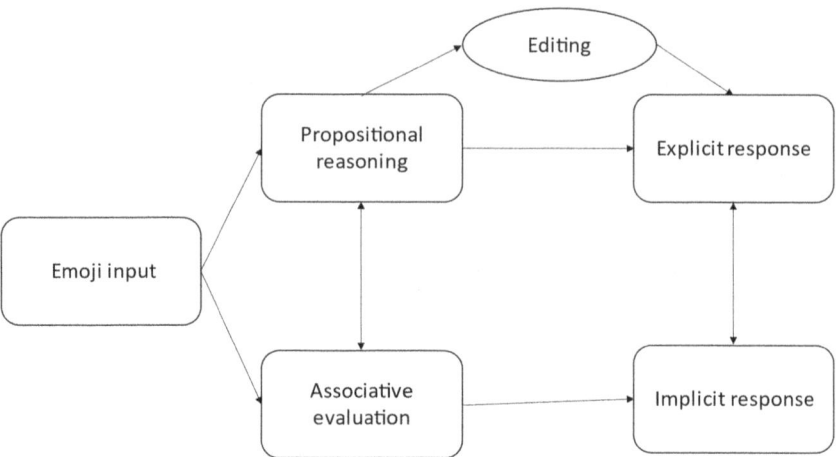

Fig. 3.1 The Associative-Propositional Evaluation Model when being applied to emoji valence evaluations

therefore bringing on long-term adaptive benefits. If we theorise positive and negative emotion on a continuum, we expect an inverted-U for positive and negative emotion to function on cognitive and behavioural responding.

This theory could have some value for researchers seeking to ask questions about how emoji might behave in respect of these principles. That is, if sad emoji really are experienced as sadness, their presentation should elicit an equivalent short-circuit to behavioural responding, whereby participants may respond more efficiently or prominently to those relative to control stimuli. This could be measured with the use of implicit response measures similar to what has been previously suggested, but might also be suited to some tasks which measure action tendencies, discussed in the following section.

Reinforcement Sensitivity Theory (RST; Gray, 1982, 1987)

To operationalise the notion of action tendencies as outlined in Broaden-and-Build theory, utilising insights from the field of action tendencies might be helpful. Typically, emotion is said to be a reaction to a specific stimulus which may prompt particular action tendencies, such as engagement with or avoidance of a target. This reaction may manifest into various different types of outputs such as a feeling, change in behaviour, facial expression or impact on the nervous system (Barrett, 2006; Lang, 1995).

In the case of positive and negative emotion, we might expect different types of action tendencies or activations as underpinned by Reinforcement sensitivity theory (RST; Gray, 1982, 1987). RST posits there to be two mechanisms which regulate emotions and behaviour. These are the Behavioural Activation System (BAS) and Behavioural Inhibition System (BIS). These vary in respect of different motivational systems that help prepare responses to significant emotional stimuli (Lang et al., 1990). The BAS is an appetitive motivational system which directs an approach to positively valenced stimuli, compared to the BIS which is a defensive motivational system that primes avoidance behaviour from negatively valenced stimuli. As such, the BAS is typically associated with positive emotions and the BIS with negative ones. More specifically, the BAS responds to rewarding stimuli which activates the response whereas the BIS responds to non-reward or punishment stimuli and decreases behavioural responses (i.e., avoidance-based behaviours) as a means of avoiding negative consequences. Behavioural inhibition broadly refers to the physiological "hard wiring" which might elicit experiences of caution in unfamiliar situations.

In respect of the BAS, useful measures might include Approach-Avoidance Tasks (AAT), physiological or arousal responses such as heart rate and the use of Functional Near-Infrared Spectroscopy (fNIRS) to measure bilateral premotor activation. Conversely, to explore aspects of BIS, this can be measured through experimental tasks such as the Go/No-Go task. These methodologies and measurements are detailed further in Chap. 4.

In the case of emoji, no research to date has empirically tested the extent to which these serve as rewarding (positively valenced emoji) vs non-rewarding (negatively valenced emoji) stimuli in respect of approach-avoidance tendencies. Some research, however, has tested physiological correlates based on emoji valence and whether these elicit differentials in acoustic startle responses (Aluja et al., 2020), skin conductance responses, heart rate and zygomatic muscle activity (Gantiva et al., 2021). This evidence suggests that unpleasant (negatively-valenced) emoji elicit heightened startle responses compared to pleasant ones, and happy emoji generate greater skin conductance response and higher zygomatic muscle activity (facial muscle activity used in smiling) relative to neutral or angry ones (Gantiva et al., 2021).

In respect of approach and avoidance, if emoji are indeed symbolic of their respective emotion concepts, we should expect to see equivalent outcomes for these tendencies to other rewarding vs non-rewarding stimuli such as words (Citron et al., 2014). Specifically, Citron et al. (2014) showed evidence of greater neural activation within the right insular cortex to word stimuli with incongruent approach-avoidance tendencies (positive high-arousal paired with negative low-arousal) relative to congruent approach-avoidance pairings (positive low-arousal words with negative high-arousal). As such, this would be a useful theoretical framework to adopt to develop an empirical area of enquiry on the behavioural approach-avoidance tendencies associated with emoji, in the case that emoji are being proposed as symbolic of emotion concepts. For example, this could have potential commercial implications in the case that findings indicate that positive-valence might stimulate associations with an approach towards certain stimuli (e.g., products, brands). In the context of e-commerce or digital marketing, the use of emoji here could potentially be highly pragmatic and bring reputational or financial gains.

Cognitive Processing of emoji

Lakoff and Johnson's (1980) Conceptual Metaphor Theory

The general principle of Lakoff and Johnson's (1980) Conceptual Metaphor Theory (CMT) is that our conceptual systems are metaphorical in nature and that metaphors influence our thinking and actions. It is argued that whilst language is used to express metaphors, these linguistic components are simply "surface manifestations" of an underlying system of conceptual thought.

In respect of abstract concepts, CMT posits that these might be structured by conceptual metaphors. For example, the concept of "love" might be readily embodied in various metaphors, including being a journey (e.g., "We have come so far in our relationship") or being a force (e.g., "I was swept off my feet"). As such, these reflect the way concepts are represented in metaphorical thought and equally can apply to conceptual domains such as emotions (Kovecses, 2000).

Given that emoji are readily considered to be symbols which represent emotion, it is intriguing to consider the extent to which we afford conceptual thought to them in this regard. That is, does a happy emoji actually correspond to the concept of happiness, and to what extent might this concept operate in an equivalent way to how emotions more generally have been proposed to function within metaphors? Exploring questions relating to this, underpinned by CMT would be a helpful advancement to the literature and contribute to the ongoing debates about the extent to which emoji are actually emotional.

Barsalou's (1999) Perceptual Symbol Systems Framework

Specifically in respect of understanding the cognitive processing aspects of emoji, a relevant theoretical framework which could be applied is the perceptual symbol systems framework (Barsalou, 1999). This theory states that conceptual knowledge incorporates different types of sensorimotor and affective information (e.g., visual features, auditory information), and therefore, this knowledge is processed through a variety of channels. For words that represent concrete concepts (e.g., fire, sun), scholars argue that recognition of these words activates perceptual or sensorimotor-related processing, which might mirror the processes that are afforded when we are actually experiencing the entity (Barsalou, 1999; Ostarek & Vigliocco, 2017; Treccani et al., 2019; for a review, see Meteyard et al., 2012). For the words "fire" and "sun" this might draw on tactile sensory processes (e.g., warmth), which supports semantic activation and processing of these concepts.

Emoji might be hypothesised to be symbols which activate perceptual, affective and/or sensory processing and therefore might support semantic categorisation/binding and inferences represented within communication. That is, if a happy emoji is posited to be representative of happiness, using this as a symbol in "happy" communication might prime affective processing, which is helpful towards the receiver's inferences within the communicative exchange.

This theoretical framework could be utilised by researchers who wish to explore the extent to which emoji are symbolic of emotion concepts (or indeed other concepts), and their role within semantic processing, particularly in relation to understanding their sensorimotor properties. However, other processing models hold relevance when understanding the semantic encoding process that might be afforded to emoji, which are discussed next. Specifically, these relate to the way emoji might provide a superior effect in respect of semantic processing compared to (or in some cases, in correspondence with) words.

Sensory-Semantic Model (Nelson, 1979)

The sensory-semantic model (Nelson, 1979) suggests that images hold advantages over words in respect of our encoding processes, known as the "picture superiority effect" (Nelson, 1979). Specifically, they are posited to be able to help us more efficiently access semantic representations than words and also consist of deeper levels of processing at the semantic level (Intraub & Nicklos, 1985; Nelson et al., 1977; Smith & Magee, 1980). Within this, stimuli are argued to be represented in long-term memory in respect of different features: semantic features (meaning, conceptual), visual (appearance) and phonemic (sound, acoustic). This model assumes that these distinct features are processed differentially based on whether the stimuli/information is verbal or non-verbal. That is, unlike words which might be labelled without accessing a semantic label (via semantic features), images require access to semantic "meaning-making" before being labelled. The sensory-semantic model therefore explains the advantages of processing images versus words through the distinctive encoding process which might be afforded to images compared to words (Nelson et al., 1976; Childers & Houston, 1983). Evidence in support of this model has found that pictures are semantically categorised more quickly than words (Smith & Magee, 1980). This presents an intriguing notion for the role of emoji within written discourse. That is, do emoji, as candidates akin to pictures/images hold an equivalent "emoji superiority effect"?

Interestingly, research which has tested this assertion has found that in the presence of congruent versus incongruent accompanying words, emoji appear to hold more difficulty than words in semantic retrieval (Paggio & Tse, 2022; Tang et al., 2020). Conversely, other evidence points to the role of emoji within semantic processing, and how this might support semantic binding and/or efficacy of semantic processing (Barach et al., 2021; Robus et al., 2020). This however has not specifically tested the memorability of semantic concepts but instead focused on eye gaze behaviour as a proxy for assuming semantic processing. However, this theoretical framework could benefit further empirical enquiry into the extent to which variations in emoji features such as quantity of visual features or the extent to which they represent different concepts might have greater or less superior effect within semantic processing.

Dual Coding Model (Paivio, 1971)

When considering how emoji might be semantically processed alongside written language, the Dual Coding Model (Paivio, 1971) holds some relevance. This model posits there to be distinguishable systems which process non-verbal imagery and linguistic/verbal information, whereby the processing of these distinct types of information becomes interconnected for encoding and retrieval of information (Paivio & Csapo, 1973). As such, the combination of these distinct types of information is said to enhance activation and thus have an addictive effect on semantic retrieval. Through various encoding and activation phases, the general result is that associative processing can occur whereby connections are made between the non-verbal and verbal information and conceptual knowledge in long-term memory. Non-verbal information (e.g., images) is said to be especially well suited to parallel processing of visual features whereas verbal might be more aligned to sequential processing.

In respect of emoji, this might be a helpful theoretical framework to understand emoji processing when used in correspondence with written language. Outcomes associated with this would include greater memorability of emoji compared to their word counterparts, or greater memorability of target words/sentences when accompanied by emoji relative to non-emoji controls. Indeed, evidence has been found that is supportive of the idea that emoji engages dual coding via the verbal and visuo-spatial systems and brings about greater memorability compared to words (Homann et al., 2022).

However, underpinned by the assertions of Paivio (1969) and based on evidence from Wicke and Bologneis (2020), this is likely to vary based on what type of emoji are used and whether they represent abstract concepts (e.g., facial emoji depicting emotional expression) versus concrete concepts (e.g., a car emoji representing a car). However, for the former (which is the primary focus of this book), given other evidence that emoji do not appear to be strongly associatively linked to emotion concepts, it is questionable as to whether a "picture superiority effect" (or perhaps an "emoji superiority effect") would occur in semantic retrieval of information relating to emotion. However, there are additional questions here about how other types of emoji such as those representing concrete concepts might hold some semantic processing advantages.

Prototypical Model of Picture and Word Processing
(Snodgrass, 1980)

A further cognitive model which holds relevance to semantic processing of emoji is the Prototypical Model of Picture and Word Processing (Snodgrass, 1980). This has resembling features to the aforementioned theoretical models. That is, this model includes three levels of processing which consist of features of process models of memory (e.g., Craik & Lockhart, 1972) and structural models of memory (e.g., Atkinson & Shiffrin, 1971). On the first level, this is said to process the physical characteristics of the information/stimulus, which moves to the second level that corresponds the feature-level information (bottom-up process) to existing prototypical information stored in long-term memory (top-down process). Finally, the third level is the propositional store of semantic knowledge which can be accessed by applying the prototypical templates from the second level.

In respect of processing images rather than words, this model explains the picture superiority effect to occur due to the fact that images hold much greater visual variability compared to words, therefore enabling more diverse variability in prototypical templates. Also, this effect may also be due to superior semantic and sensory codes which might be afforded to images versus words (Snodgrass & Asieghi, 1977).

Similar to the aforementioned cognitive models, in respect of emoji, applying this framework would present an intriguing proof of concept. That is, it is not overly apparent as to whether emoji might hold prototypical representations which would facilitate such an effect. Empirical evidence to test these assertions could approach this using a "learning" or "training" approach which might typically be used in psycholinguistic or language acquisition research. This could ask participants to learn names which are presented alongside novel emoji and test the extent to which learnt emoji (which hold prototypical representations) might be processed more effectively or efficiently than non-learnt stimuli.

To summarise the theoretical frameworks relating to the cognitive processing of emoji, these generally present opportunities to operationalise the nature by which emoji might draw upon the semantic system, and whether this works in parallel or in distinctive ways to the processing of word counterparts. Given claims about the multimodality of emoji, this raises intriguing questions about potential interaction of how the verbal and non-verbal properties of emoji are represented semantically and how this relates to how they are encoded and retrieved within semantic processing. Another level here is the extent to which any affective components of emoji feature in this process.

INTERPERSONAL PROCESSING OF EMOJI

Social Information Processing Theory (Walther, 1992)

Within the field of computer-mediated communication (CMC), the seminal work of Walther (1992) noted how our interactions and exchanges within online contexts serve relatively equivalent functions to in-person ones to help us obtain social information and support interpersonal processes. Social Information Processing Theory posits that we use behavioural cues from others as a means of developing relationships and understanding the perspective of others (Walther, 1992; Walther & D'Addario, 2001). Moreover, from this was derived the hyperpersonal model of communication (Walther, 1996) which outlines that online-based communication in some cases may surpass offline equivalents in respect of the way we might have a tendency to overcompensate for the typical absence of non-verbal cues. Specifically, less rich or natural media (as per Media Richness Theory and Media Naturalness Theory, discussed below) may permit greater attention to carefully crafted exchanges which might be perceived more favourably. Within this theoretical framework, emoji would be considered paralinguistic/non-verbal cues which serve as a part of increasing the richness of what might typically be "less rich" communicative exchanges and thus support relationship development. Indeed, this has been found to be the case (Gesselman et al., 2019), although some key considerations are warranted on the generalisability of these principles (Cavalheiro et al., 2024). Namely, the nature of communication outcomes of using emoji on relationships or perceptions of others is likely to vary based on the specific type of emoji used and the dynamics of the interaction (e.g., high conflict versus low) (Cavalheiro et al., 2024). As such, the extent to which emoji facilitate and/or enrich text-based forms of communication will be somewhat context-specific and unlikely to hold universal interpersonal outcomes.

Emotion as Social Information Model (EASI; Van Kleef, 2009)

The Emotion as Social Information Model (EASI; Van Kleef, 2009) posits that social interactions and behaviour are, in part, mediated by emotional expression. More specifically, the nature of the receiver's emotional reaction can be influenced by their inferential processing based on their perception of the sender's mood state or relational orientation. In the context of emoji, this might suggest that in cases where these are being used as markers of emotional expression, it might aid the social information processing bandwidth and/or capacity of the receiver/s to draw inferences about the interpersonal interaction. Interestingly, there is a paucity of research which has explicitly tested the EASI model within CMC and specifically in the study of emoji. However, given that emoji are often reported to be used as a way of overcoming the absence of non-verbal cues within text-based online communication (Aldunate & González-Ibáñez, 2017; Aldunate et al., 2018; Derks et al., 2008, 2008), this could be a relevant theoretical framework to more readily apply to the psychological study of emoji.

What could be especially intriguing to explore here is the extent to which perspective-taking might operate in this regard. That is, if the receiver's inferences are central to the EASI model's principles, there is something relevant to test here about how the receiver's *proficiency* in perspective-taking plays a role in the success of an interaction. A receiver who has well-attuned perspective-taking might be well equipped to understand the perspectives or intentions of the sender in their use of a specific emoji to represent a specific concept. This might help create a shared concept of the meaning of a given emoji for those interaction partners.

As there is often a lack of universality in the labels afforded to emoji, perspective-taking abilities might be especially relevant in the way we create shared representations of emoji concepts between interaction partners, for example, "Because I believe that you are using emoji X to represent concept X, then I will use this knowledge to interpret your message. I will then also use emoji X to represent concept X during my interactions with you as I believe this will help you interpret the intended meaning from my messages" (See Fig. 3.2 for an example). This perspective-taking therefore creates a shared usage of emoji X to represent concept X in the context of this interaction, which would not necessarily be possible if the original receiver was not able to understand the intentions or perspectives of the original sender. Intriguingly, this does not appear to be a well-established avenue within the emoji research literature, despite it posing some interesting questions.

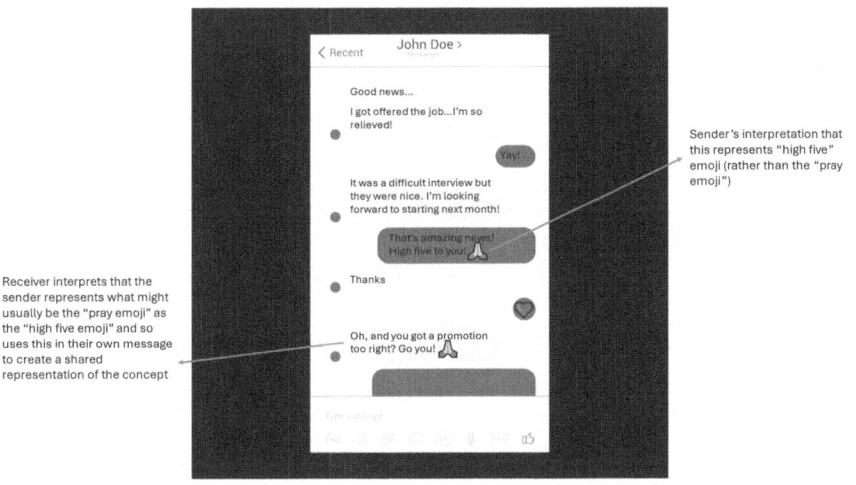

Receiver interprets that the sender represents what might usually be the "pray emoji" as the "high five emoji" and so uses this in their own message to create a shared representation of the concept

Sender's interpretation that this represents "high five" emoji (rather than the "pray emoji")

this figure will be printed in b/w

Fig. 3.2 Example of how shared representations of emoji might be created

Media Richness Theory (Daft & Lengel, 1986)

For scholars who may approach the study of emoji as part of social or interpersonal communication (largely those who might work in fields such as communication or media studies), Media Richness Theory posits that the receiver's processing or understanding of a message is influenced primarily by the richness of the way it is presented (Daft & Lengel, 1986). Messages which can extend the perceptual bandwidth such as via multimodal communication (e.g., concurrent visual and audio modalities) are said to be higher in richness than communications which might be unimodal or text-based (Wang et al., 2023a, b). Four key factors are said to determine the level of media richness: (1) number of cues being used to convey a message; (2) number of meanings which can be expressed through symbols used; (3) how quickly responses can be issued; and (4) level of personalisation within the message (Daft et al., 1987).

In respect of emoji, these have been proposed to enhance the richness of text-based messages (Sheer & Chen, 2004). To give illustrative examples from the literature, studies using this framework have explored how the combination of text content and visual content in the form of emoji might impact user engagement in online interactions (McShane et al., 2021; Wang et al., 2023a, b). However, one of the challenges of research which has utilised this model as a framework is that it is not easily distinguishable how each of the four aforementioned factors are operationalised in research, and therefore what constituent aspect of "richness" emoji corresponds to. Whilst it is arguably the case that they map directly to the factor of increasing the number of cues, they may also correspond to other factors including the number of meanings and even level of personalisation. As such, it is not clear from this research how emoji align to specific aspects of richness, and therefore whether it is the perceptual or conceptual bandwidth (or both) that emoji might be enhancing. Therefore, some more intricate research is needed which is better placed to identify more specifically the mechanisms behind these principles.

Media Naturalness Theory (Kock, 2005, 2011)

Somewhat related to Media Richness Theory is Media Naturalness Theory (Kock, 2005, 2011), which broadly builds on the aforementioned principles. A key distinction here, however, is that this refers to the extent to which the behaviour encompassed within a message aligns with what is considered to meet natural communication characteristics. Here, behaviour which mirrors face-to-face communication would be argued to be the "gold standard" of natural communication relative to other derivates of communication, such as text-based exchanges. This focuses on five elements of (1) high levels of co-location, (2) synchronicity, (3) ability to express and observe facial expressions, (4) ability to express and observe body language and (5) ability to express and listen to speech.

The focus in Media Naturalness Theory is on behaviour itself, which exists within the message exchange rather than the richness of the platform or channel by which this behaviour is being communicated. Arguably, media richness and naturalness tend to be strongly associated, but there can be instances in which the underpinning behaviour is represented distinctly within a computer-mediated communicative exchange (Kaye et al., 2022). A good example of this is behaviour which might be entirely natural such as walking behaviour, which is represented in statistics or map metrics on fitness apps. Here, the underpinning behaviour is natural but the message by which it is communicated lacks equivalent richness. The consequences of this are said to have differential effects, whereby less natural behaviour draws upon greater cognitive resources, and this can bring on additional cognitive load within processing (Kock, 2004). Expanded further from this is Media Compensation Theory (Hantula et al., 2011), which posits that users may use cues such as emoji as a means of compensating for the cues which might usually exist within face-to-face communication (e.g., tone of voice, facial expression). As such, they use these as a way to aid naturalness and equivalency.

In respect of emoji, whilst their paralinguistic properties have been widely recognised, it is not fully clear the extent to which they might increase naturalness in CMC. Tangentially, they have been noted to increase perceptions of social presence (Cavalheiro et al., n.d., under review), which might in some way mimic the perception of being co-located. However, there is no compelling evidence which fully establishes how they are either used or processed in a way which is thought to increase "naturalness" in communication. Indeed, some years ago, we noted that digital communications might be more considered and consciously controlled than traditional face-to-face expressions (Kaye et al., 2017). Additionally, as emoji can only be accessed via an interaction with a digital device or platform, this raises another query about the extent to which interactivity with hardware itself features in the "naturalness" continuum. Channel Expansion Theory (Carlson & Zmud, 1999) however might offer some potential insights into this latter query, discussed next.

Channel Expansion Theory (Carlson & Zmud, 1999)

Extending further from the aforementioned theories, Channel Expansion Theory (Carlson & Zmud, 1999) emphasises the role of the receiver and their perceptions of media richness. More specifically, this posits that through experience/expertise with a communication platform, users acquire and enrich their capabilities and perceptual affordances of it (D'Urso, 2020). That is, the more experience a user has with using a specific channel or platform of communication, the richer they perceive it to be. Four elements are discussed as being relevant here: (1) experience with the channel, (2) experience with the message topic, (3) experience with the context and (4) experience with the communication partner. Essentially, this theory recognises the interaction of social and cognitive elements of processing which might be relevant to understand the receiver's processing of online messages.

In the context of emoji, this might be a more helpful basis than aforementioned "naturalness" approaches as there is some recognition of the role of the interface and user experience aspects within the communicational exchange. Arguably, the role of hardware (i.e., devices) and software (e.g., social media platforms, Unicode integration etc) determine the way we are able to select (sender) and render (receiver) emoji within our interactions. As such, understanding the device-level and software-level interactions are important for exploring the affordances associated with how we process emoji. These affordances are not so explicitly recognised in other theoretical frameworks, and so Channel Expansion Theory perhaps contributes some novel insight here to provide a more comprehensive CMC perspective for emoji processing.

Funder's Realistic Accuracy Model (Funder, 1995, 1999)

Within the interpersonal perception literature, it is widely acknowledged that the context and behaviour of others serve as important cues in our impression formation of others (Letzring et al., 2006; Wall et al., 2016). Funder's Realistic Accuracy Model (Funder, 1995, 1999) provides a framework to explain the way we interpret the behaviour of others and utilise this to form (accurate) impressions of them. Specifically, this outlines four processes which inform how we may form accurate trait-specific judgements of others, specifically at first impression. Firstly, the behaviour being displayed must be *relevant* to the specific trait being judged, and secondly, be *available* (visible) to the person making the judgement. Thirdly, the behaviour must be *detected* and finally *utilised* accordingly in the judgement-making process. A pragmatic approach within this area of enquiry suggests "perception is for doing" (Gibson, 1979), whereby perceptions may be utilised and serve useful outcomes for the person making the judgement (e.g., improves the relationship with the person, helps them decide whether to employ them for a job).

This theoretical framework has utility for scholars interested in exploring or explaining the extent to which emoji function within interactional behaviours or relationship formation/maintenance. Indeed, previous research has applied this to the study of emoji (Kaye et al., 2020; Wall et al., 2016). Particularly within commercial or business contexts, this could be especially fruitful. For example, pragmatic outcomes of using emoji within brand-consumer communications could be brand reputation or increased online sales. Within organisational culture, using emoji online or distributed working could enhance employee connection or relationships. In relation to the wider field of interpersonal perception, this might offer some conceptual advancement of understanding how judgement accuracy relates not only to people but brands and organisations.

Elaboration Likelihood Model (Petty & Cacioppo, 1986)

The Elaboration Likelihood Model (ELM; Petty & Cacioppo, 1986) broadly is a theory relating to attitude change and the processes involved in persuasive communication. Whilst this typically is not a widely used theoretical framework afforded to the study of emoji, there are principles within this which I argue are relevant. The ELM posits there to be two routes to persuasion: central route and peripheral route (Petty & Cacioppo, 1986). Whilst the central route broadly consists of the logical, reasoned aspects of processing a message, the peripheral route is characterised by heuristic-based processing (ibid). Emoji might be an interesting candidate here to prime heuristics, whereby they may serve as indicators of sentiment ("this feels good") and thus short-cut the process of the receiver fully (or logically) processing the message. This assertion is supported by research which has tested the impact of emoji on consumer perceptions and the processing of restaurant reports/reviews (Ray & Merle, 2021). Specifically, positive-valenced emoji have been found to decrease the likelihood of the content of the restaurant reports being elaborated (i.e., centrally) and therefore appear to short-circuit processing.

There is a wide range of fruitful contexts which can be considered here, such as within health or political communication or commercial marketing (Distel et al., 2022). In respect of online health communication, research has found that narrative messages which include emoji (relative to those which do not) increase message credibility but also increase message elaboration (Willoughby & Lu, 2018). Arguably, the use (and effectiveness) of emoji is likely to vary based on factors such as features of the message (content and goals of message) as well as the resulting outcomes from this (call to action for a "real world behaviour" vs online-based behaviour). As such, whilst the evidence suggests that emoji may be indicators that both enhance and diminish elaboration of central message content, the nature of this effect is largely influenced by a variety of other factors; therefore, it is not possible to draw universal conclusions about how emoji may support persuasive tendencies towards attitude or behaviour change.

SUMMARY

A key limitation of a large majority of research is a lack of relevant or coherent theoretical framework to underpin programmes of research on emoji. As such, a large majority of studies have not been guided by a theoretical framework from which to correspond to existing (and in many cases, very well established) theoretical ideas and evidence bases. This has resulted in much of the emoji research being represented somewhat disparately from relevant literature and what I suspect is partially the reason why there has been little synthesis in this field, to date.

If I was to synthesise more specifically, this would be my take-home insights about the general theoretical approaches used. The research literature exploring the emotional functions of emoji in general appears to have not capitalised so strongly on theoretical frameworks. Whilst my own research and planned projects are typically aligned to some of the theoretical principles outlined within this theme, it appears there are a range of well-established theoretical ideas here which could be exploited far more explicitly and widely in research programmes exploring the emotional functions of emoji. Similarly, research which sits within cognitive processing has a wide range of robust theoretical models but many of these have not explicitly been underpinning principles which have driven research. This in itself can present some limitations on the extent to which cyberpsychology insights can be considered "significant" in respect of Research Excellence Framework (REF) exercises which seek to situate findings based on their conceptual contributions in their wider discipline. On the other hand, research on interpersonal processing has been much more explicit in applying key theories, and these have been a basis for selecting testable research questions/hypotheses and informing methodological approaches. However, in many cases, it has not always determined the relative strength or influence of each of the principles outlined in the respective theories towards increasing richness or naturalness within CMC. As such, perhaps more intricate methodological approaches could be useful here to more fully explore these.

Within this chapter, I have outlined a number of relevant theoretical frameworks and provided insight into how these may correspond to lines of enquiry relating to the processing of emoji. What is particularly evident is that these can be used by researchers representing a wide range of domains and specialisms, which I argue can only serve to enrich the empirical study of emoji.

REFERENCES

Aldunate, N., & González-Ibáñez, R. (2017). An integrated review of emoticons in computer-mediated communication. *Frontiers in Psychology, 7,* 1–6. https://doi.org/10.3389/fpsyg.2016.02061

Aldunate, N., Villena-González, M., Rojas-Thomas, F., López, V., & Bosman, C. A. (2018). Mood detection in ambiguous messages: The interaction between text and emoticons. *Frontiers in Psychology, 9.* https://doi.org/10.3389/fpsyg.2018.00423

Aluja, A., Balada, F., Blanco, E., Lucas, I., & Blanch, A. (2020). Startle reflex modulation by affective face "Emoji" pictographs. *Psychological Research, 84,* 15–22. https://doi.org/10.1007/s00426-018-0991-x

Atkinson, R. C., & Shiffrin, R. M. (1971). The control of short term memory. *Scientific American, 225*(2), 82–90. https://doi.org/10.1038/scientificamerican0871-82

Barach, E., Feldman, L. B., & Sheridan, H. (2021). Are emojis processed like words?: Eye movements reveal the time course of semantic processing for emojified text. *Psychonomic Bulletin Review, 28,* 978–991. https://doi.org/10.3758/s13423-020-01864-y

Barrett, L. F. (2006). Are emotions natural kinds? *Perspectives on Psychological Science, 1*(1), 28–58. https://doi.org/10.1111/j.1745-6916.2006.00003.x

Barsalou, L. W. (1999). Perceptual symbol systems. *Behavioral and Brain Sciences, 22,* 577–660. https://doi.org/10.1017/s0140525x99002149

Carlson, J. R., & Zmud, R. W. (1999). Channel expansion theory and the experiential nature of media richness perceptions. *Academy of Management Journal, 42*(2), 153–170. https://doi.org/10.2307/257090

Cavalheiro, B. P., Prada, M., & Rodrigues, D. L. (2024). Examining the effects of reciprocal emoji use on interpersonal and communication outcomes. *Journal of Social and Personal Relationships.* https://doi.org/10.1177/02654075231219

Cavalheiro, B. P., Prada, M., & Rodrigues, D. L. (n.d.). *Show yourself?! Social presence as a mechanism for the effects of using different pictorial cues in text-based computer-mediated communication.*

Childers, T. L., & Houston, M. J. (1983). Imagery paradigms for consumer research: Alternative perspectives from cognitive psychology. In R. P. Bagozzi & A. M. Tybout (Eds.), *Advances in consumer research* (pp. 59–64). Association for Consumer Research.

Citron, F. M. M., Gray, M. A., Critchley, H. D., & Weekes, B. S. (2014). Emotional valence and arousal affect reading in an interactive way: Neuroimaging evidence for an approach-withdrawal framework. *Neuropsychologia, 56,* 79–89. https://doi.org/10.1016/j.neuropsychologia.2014.01.002

Craik, F. I. M., & Lockhart, R. S. (1972). Levels of processing: A framework for memory research. *Journal of Verbal Learning and Verbal Behavior, 11*(6), 671–684. https://doi.org/10.1016/S0022-5371(72)80001-X

D'Urso, S. C. (2020). Channel expansion theory. In J. Bulck (Ed.), *The international encyclopedia of media psychology* (1st ed., pp. 1–6). Wiley. https://doi.org/10.1002/9781119011071.iemp0119

Daft, R. L., & Lengel, R. H. (1986). Organizational information requirements, media richness and structural design. *Management Science, 32*(5), 554–571. https://doi.org/10.1287/mnsc.32.5.554

Daft, R. L., Lengel, R. H., & Trevino, L. K. (1987). Message equivocality, media selection, and manager performance: Implications for information systems. *MIS Quarterly, 11*(3), 355–366. https://doi.org/10.2307/248682

Derks, D., Bos, A. E. R., & Von Grumbkow, J. (2008). Emoticons and online message interpretation. *Social Science Computer Review, 26*(3), 379–388. https://doi.org/10.1177/0894439307311611

Derks, D., Fischer, A. H., & Bos, A. E. R. (2008). The role of emotion in computer-mediated communication: A review. *Computers in Human Behavior, 24*(3), 766–785. https://doi.org/10.1016/j.chb.2007.04.004

Distel, V., Egger, R., Petrovic, U., Phan, V. L., & Wiesinger, S. (2022). The usage of emoji in tourism-related Instagram posts: Suggestions from a marketing perspective. In J. L. Stienmetz, B. Ferrer-Rosell, & D. Massimo (Eds.), *Information and communication technologies in tourism 2022. Proceedings of the ENTER 2022 eTourism conference, 11–14 January.* Springer.

Fredrickson, B. L. (1998). What good are positive emotions? *Review of General Psychology, 2*, 300–319. https://doi.org/10.1037/1089-2680.2.3.300

Fredrickson, B. L. (2001). The role of positive emotions in positive psychology. The broaden-and-build theory of positive emotions. *American Psychologist, 56*(3), 218–226. https://doi.org/10.1037/0003-066x.56.3.218

Funder, D. C. (1995). On the accuracy of personality judgment: A realistic approach. *Psychological Review, 102*(4), 652. https://doi.org/10.1037/0033-295x.102.4.652

Funder, D. C. (1999). *Personality judgment: A realistic approach to person perception.* Academic Press.

Gantiva, C., Araujo, A., Castillo, K., Claor, L., & Hurtado-Parrado, C. (2021). Physiological and affective responses to emoji faces: Effects on facial muscle activity, skin conductance, heart rate, and self-reported affect. *Biological Psychology, 163*, 108142. https://doi.org/10.1016/j.biopsycho.2021.108142

Gawronski, B., & Bodenhausen, G. V. (2006). Associative and propositional processes in evaluation: An integrative review of implicit and explicit attitude change. *Psychological Bulletin, 132*, 692–731. https://doi.org/10.1037/0033-2909.132.5.692

Gawronski, B., & Bodenhausen, G. V. (2007). Unraveling the processes underlying evaluation: Attitudes from the perspective of the APE model. *Social Cognition, 25*, 687–717.

Gawronski, B., & Bodenhausen, G. V. (2009). Operating principles versus operating conditions in the distinction between associative and propositional processes. *Behavioral and Brain Sciences, 32*, 183–246. https://doi.org/10.1017/S0140525X09000855

Gawronski, B., & Bodenhausen, G. V. (2011). The Associative–Propositional evaluation model: Theory, evidence, and open questions. *Advances in Experimental Social Psychology, 44.* https://doi.org/10.1016/B978-0-12-385522-0.00002-0

Gesselman, A. N., Ta-Johnson, V. P., & Garcia, J. R. (2019). Worth a thousand interpersonal words: Emoji as affective signals for relationship-oriented digital communication. *PLoS One, 14*(8), e0221297. https://doi.org/10.1371/journal.pone.0221297

Gibson, J. J. (1979). *The ecological approach to perception.* Lawrence Erlbaum Associates.

Gray, J. A. (1982). *The neuropsychology of anxiety: An enquiry into the functions of the septo-hippocampal system.* Clarendon Press.

Gray, J. A. (1987). The neuropsychology of emotion and personality. In S. M. Stahl, S. D. Iverson, & E. C. Goodman (Eds.), *Cognitive neurochemistry* (pp. 171–190). Oxford University Press.

Hantula, D. A., Kock, N., D'Arcy, J. P., & DeRosa, D. M. (2011). Media compensation theory: A Darwinian perspective on adaptation to electronic communication and collaboration. In G. Saad (Ed.), *Evolutionary psychology in the business sciences* (pp. 339–363). Springer. https://doi.org/10.1007/978-3-540-92784-6_13

Homann, L. A., Roberts, B. R. T., Ahmed, S., & Fernandes, M. A. (2022). Are emojis processed visuo-spatially or verbally? Evidence for dual codes. *Visual Cognition, 30*(4), 267–279. https://doi.org/10.1080/13506285.2022.2050871

Intraub, H., & Nicklos, S. (1985). Levels of processing and picture memory: The physical superiority effect. *Journal of Experimental Psychology. Learning, Memory, and Cognition, 11*, 284–298. https://doi.org/10.1037/0278-7393.11.2.284

Kaye, L. K., Malone, S. A., & Wall, H. J. (2017). Emojis: Insights, affordances and possibilities for psychological science. *Trends in Cognitive Sciences, 21*(2), 66–68. https://doi.org/10.1016/j.tics.2016.10.007

Kaye, L. K., Rousaki, A., Joyner, L. C., Barrett, L. A. F., & Orchard, L. J. (2022). The online behaviour taxonomy: A conceptual framework to understand behaviour in computer-mediated communication. *Computers in Human Behavior, 137*, 107443. https://doi.org/10.1016/j.chb.2022.107443

Kaye, L. K., Wall, H. J., & Hird, A. T. (2020). Less is more when rating extraversion: Behavioural cues and interpersonal perceptions on the platform of Facebook. *Psychology of Popular Media, 9*(4), 465–474. https://doi.org/10.1037/ppm0000263

Kock, N. (2004). The psychobiological model: Towards a new theory of computer-mediated communication based on Darwinian evolution. *Organization Science, 15*(3), 327–348. https://doi.org/10.1287/orsc.1040.0071

Kock, N. (2005). Media richness or media naturalness? The evolution of our biological communication apparatus and its influence on our behavior toward E-communication tools. *IEEE Transactions on Professional Communication, 48*(2), 117–130. https://doi.org/10.1109/TPC.2005.849649

Kock, N. (2011). Media naturalness theory: Human evolution and behaviour towards electronic communication technologies. In S. C. Roberts (Ed.), *Applied evolutionary psychology* (pp. 380–398). Oxford University Press. https://doi.org/10.1093/acprof:oso/9780199586073.003.0023

Kovecses, Z. (2000). *Metaphor and emotion.* Cambridge University Press.

Lakoff, G., & Johnson, M. (1980). *Metaphors we live by.* University of Chicago Press.

Lang, P. J. (1995). The emotion probe: Studies of motivation and attention. *American Psychologist, 50*(5), 372–385. https://doi.org/10.1037/0003-066X.50.5.372

Lang, P. J., Bradley, M. M., & Cuthbert, B. N. (1990). Emotion, attention, and the startle reflex. *Psychological Review, 97*(3), 377–395. https://doi.org/10.1037/0033-295X.97.3.377

Letzring, T. D., Wells, S. M., & Funder, D. C. (2006). Information quantity and quality affect the realistic accuracy of personality judgment. *Journal of Personality and Social Psychology, 91*(1), 111–123. https://doi.org/10.1037/0022-3514.91.1.111

McShane, L., Pancer, E., Poole, M., & Deng, Q. (2021). Emoji, playfulness, and brand engagement on twitter. *Journal of Interactive Marketing, 53*(1), 96–110.

Meteyard, L., Rodriguez-Cuadrado, S., Bahrami, B., & Vigliocco, G. (2012). Coming of age: A review of embodiment and the neuroscience of semantics. *Cortex, 48*(7), 788–804. https://doi.org/10.1016/j.cortex.2010.11.002

Nelson, D. L. (1979). Remembering pictures and words: Appearance, significance, and name. In L. S. Cermak & F. I. M. Craik (Eds.), *Levels of processing in human memory* (pp. 45–76). Erlbaum.

Nelson, D. L., Reed, V. S., & McEvoy, C. L. (1977). Learning to order pictures and words: A model of sensory and semantic encoding. *Journal of Experimental Psychology: Human Learning and Memory, 3*, 485–497. https://doi.org/10.1037/0278-7393.3.5.485

Nelson, D. L., Reed, V. S., & Walling, J. R. (1976). The pictorial superiority effect. *Journal of Experimental Psychology: Human Learning and Memory, 9*, 523–578. https://doi.org/10.1037/0278-7393.2.5.523

Ostarek, M., & Vigliocco, G. (2017). Reading sky and seeing a cloud: On the relevance of events for perceptual simulation. *Journal of Experimental Psychology: Learning, Memory, and Cognition, 43*(4), 579–590. https://doi.org/10.1037/xlm0000318

Paggio, P., & Tse, A. P. P. (2022). Are emoji processed like words? An eye-tracking study. *Cognitive Science, 46,* e13099. https://doi.org/10.1111/cogs.13099

Paivio, A. (1969). Mental imagery in associative learning and memory. *Psychological Review, 76,* 241–263.

Paivio, A. (1971). *Imagery and verbal processes.* Holt, Rinehart and Winston.

Paivio, A., & Csapo, K. (1973). Picture superiority in free recall: Imagery or dual coding? *Cognitive Psychology, 5*(2), 176–206. https://doi.org/10.1016/0010-0285(73)90032-7

Petty, R. E., & Cacioppo, J. T. (1986). The Elaboration Likelihood Model of Persuasion. *Advances in Experimental Social Psychology, 9,* 123–205. https://doi.org/10.1016/S0065-2601(08)60214-2

Ray, E. C., & Merle, P. F. (2021). Disgusting face, disease-ridden place?: Emoji influence on the interpretation of restaurant inspection reports. *Health Communication, 36*(14), 1867–1878. https://doi.org/10.1080/10410236.2020.1802867

Robus, C. M., Hand, C. J., Filik, R., & Pitchford, M. (2020). Investigating effects of emoji on neutral narrative text: Evidence from eye movements and perceived emotional valence. *Computers in Human Behavior, 109,* 106361. https://doi.org/10.1016/j.chb.2020.106361

Sheer, V. C., & Chen, L. (2004). Improving media richness theory: A study of interaction goals, message valence, and task complexity in manager-subordinate communication. *Management Communication Quarterly, 18*(1), 76–93. https://doi.org/10.1177/0893318904265803

Smith, M. C., & Magee, L. E. (1980). Tracing the time course of picture – Word processing. *Journal of Experimental Psychology: General, 109,* 373–392. https://doi.org/10.1037/0096-3445.109.4.373

Snodgrass, J. G. (1980). Towards a model for picture and word processing. In P. A. Kolers, M. E. Wrolstad, & H. Bouma (Eds.), *Processing of visible language. Nato conference series* (Vol. 13). Springer. https://doi.org/10.1007/978-1-4684-1068-6_42

Snodgrass, J. G., & Asieghi, A. (1977). The pictorial superiority effect in recognition memory. *Bulletin of the Psychonomic Society, 10,* 1–4. https://doi.org/10.3758/BF03333530

Tang, M., Chen, B., Zhao, X., & Zhao, L. (2020). Processing network emojis in Chinese sentence context: An ERP study. *Neuroscience Letters, 722,* 134815. https://doi.org/10.1016/j.neulet.2020.134815

Treccani, B., Mulatti, C., Sulpizio, S., & Job, R. (2019). Does perceptual simulation explain spatial effects in word categorization? *Frontiers in Psychology, 10*, e1102. https://doi.org/10.3389/fpsyg.2019.01102

Van Kleef, G. A. (2009). How emotions regulate social life: The Emotions as Social Information (EASI) model. *Current Directions in Psychological Science, 18*(3), 184–188. https://doi.org/10.1111/j.1467-8721.2009.01633.x

Wall, H. J., Kaye, L. K., & Malone, S. A. (2016). An exploration of psychological factors on emoticon usage and implications for judgement accuracy. *Computers in Human Behavior, 62*, 70–78. https://doi.org/10.1016/j.chb.2016.03.040

Wall, H. J., Taylor, P. J., & Campbell, C. (2016). Getting the balance right? A mismatch in interaction demands between target and judge impacts on judgement ac curacy for some traits but not others. *Personality and Individual Differences, 88*, 66–72. https://doi.org/10.1016/j.paid.2015.08.037

Walther, J. B. (1992). Interpersonal effects in computer-mediated interaction. *Communication Research, 19*(1), 52–90. https://doi.org/10.1177/0093 65092019001003

Walther, J. B. (1996). Computer-mediated communication: Impersonal, interpersonal, and hyperpersonal interaction. *Communication Research, 23*(1), 3–43. https://doi.org/10.1177/009365096023001001

Walther, J. B., & D'Addario, K. P. (2001). The impacts of emoticons on message interpretation in computer-mediated communication. *Social Science Computer Review, 19*(3), 324–347. https://doi.org/10.1177/089443930101900307

Wang, X., Cheng, M., Zhu, J., & Jiang, R. (2023a). When texts meet emoji: A multi-stage study of tourism brands. *Journal of Travel Research.* https://doi.org/10.1177/00472875231203396

Wang, K.-Y., Chih, W.-H., & Honora, A. (2023b). How the emoji use in apology messages influences customers' responses in online service recoveries: The moderating role of communication style. *International Journal of Information Management, 69*, 102618. https://doi.org/10.1016/j.ijinfomgt.2022.102618

Wicke, P., & Bologneis, M. (2020). Emoji-based semantic representations for abstract and concrete concepts. *Cognitive Processing, 21*, 615–635.

Willoughby, J. F., & Lu, S. (2018). Do pictures help tell the story? An experimental test of narrative and emojis in a health text message intervention. *Computers in Human Behavior, 79*, 75–82. https://doi.org/10.1016/j.chb.2017.10.031

Methodological Approaches

Abstract Chapter 4 reviews the various methodological paradigms and measurements which have been used in the study of emoji processing. This is structured under implicit and explicit measures. These include Spatial Stroop tasks, Lexical and semantic decision tasks, Dot Probe tasks, eye-tracking, Approach-Avoidance tasks, Go/No-Go tasks, neuroimaging, memory retrieval tasks, perception and attitude scales, and sentiment scales. Chapter 4 provides a summary of take-away points about general findings across methodological paradigms and where opportunities may reside on how these methodological paradigms might be used to advance the study of emoji processing.

Keywords Emoji • Implicit measures • Explicit measures • Response times • Valence effects • Emoji conditions

In this chapter, we move away from the conceptual and more towards the methodological. Within this chapter, I review the range of methodological paradigms and measurements which have been used in the psychological study of emoji processing. Chapter 2 made reference to various conceptual approaches and cited some examples of methodological paradigms which might typically be used to explore these. Across the various methodological paradigms and measurements, these can be categorised as measuring

© The Author(s), under exclusive license to Springer Nature   63
Switzerland AG 2024
L. K. Kaye, *The Psychology of Emoji Processing*, Palgrave
Studies in Cyberpsychology,
https://doi.org/10.1007/978-3-031-75113-4_4

implicit processes and/or responses (spatial Stroop task, lexical decision task, Dot Probe task, Go/No-Go task, Approach-Avoidance task, eye-tracking, neuroimaging) and explicit responses (perception scales, valence evaluation scales, memory retrieval tasks).

In relation to measured outcomes associated with emoji processing, for implicit responses these can include reaction times and accuracy (via keyboard press on computerised tasks) and attentional vigilance (via eye gaze regions of interest or eye movements). For explicit responses, these can include valence evaluation (via Likert scale rating), memory retrieval tasks, and message and/or sender perceptions (via Likert scale informant reports). Whilst the methodological paradigms and measurements are arguably appropriate for the respective domain of research it is situated within, this brings about significant challenge when synthesising this as a whole. This chapter includes a detailed review of each of these key methodological paradigms/tasks to illuminate the insights these have afforded the psychological study of emoji.

The Curious Case of the "Neutral" Emoji

Before diving into the various methodological paradigms within the study of emoji processing, it is pertinent to note an observation which has started to plague researchers in this field but also wider fields in the study of facial processing. Largely, this raises questions about whether neutral emoji are indeed actually interpreted/processed as neutral stimuli.

For context, it is rather typical in studies which experimentally test the effects of emoji to include control conditions. In the case of manipulating emoji valence, this might typically include the following conditions: positive valence and negative valence, with neutral valence operating as a control condition. However, even normative ratings of emoji which are labelled as "neutral" indicate that these tend, on average, to be rated a little below the neutral line, inclining towards the negative (Rodrigues et al., 2018). This observation has been replicated in other research which has sought to use neutral emoji as control conditions (e.g., Kaye et al., 2022). In other cases, neutral emoji have been found to hold the greatest range in "neutrality" ratings relative to positive or negative emoji, which tend not to deviate so much (Novak et al., 2015).

This poses some methodological challenges for researchers when issuing control within experimental design. Whilst normative ratings can offer some justification for researchers on the steps taken to control valence appropriately between conditions, it raises a conceptual or even a philosophical question about whether neutral emoji are actually considered neutral. Interestingly, even Reddit users have started to debate this issue (socks888, 2023)! Whilst there is not a straightforward answer to this, I wish to include this as a note of caution for scholars to be mindful of this issue, especially when designing experimental conditions which might be seeking a suitable control condition.

IMPLICIT MEASURES AND RESPONSES

There is a range of implicit measures and responses to understand how we process emoji. This section outlines each of these in turn.

Spatial Stroop Task

Chapter 2 outlined research related to spatial iconicity and its application to the study of emoji processing. A key methodological paradigm to test spatial iconicity is the Spatial Stroop Task (White, 1969). This is an experimental task which measures our abilities to negotiate any cognitive interference of a stimulus' features (Stroop, 1935; Scarpina & Tagini, 2017). For a Spatial Stroop, this more specifically tests the interference between the stimuli's symbolic features and the spatial location of its presentation (MacLeod, 1991; Wuhr, 2007). Operationally, this typically manipulates where in the visual field the stimuli are presented. As noted in Chap. 2, because there are observed valence-space interactions (e.g., positive = up, negative = down), semantic interference would be proposed to be experienced when stimuli are presented in spatial positions which are counter to those which are prototypical. This interference requires attentional resources and thus inhibits processing efficiency. Findings from this task can therefore help infer automatic or implicit aspects of processing and thus can help answer questions about how conceptual knowledge relating to emotion concepts is represented and retrieved from semantic memory.

In the case of emoji, we developed the Emoji Spatial Stroop task (Kaye et al., 2022), which provides a test case for assessing the spatial iconicity effects of emoji. The original version includes a series of trials depicting 24 emoji (eight positive, eight neutral, eight negative), which are controlled based on normative ratings of valence by Rodrigues et al. (2018). Each emoji is situated in three positions across the vertical axis on the experimental display: upper vertical position (0.5 cm from the top of the display), lower vertical position (0.5 cm from the bottom of the display) and central position (the intersection of the vertical and horizontal axis of the display). When we employed this in further studies (Kaye et al., 2023), participants engaged in a categorisation task, where they were asked to make a decision on the stimulus presented in each trial (e.g., Is this a human face?", "Is this positive?") via pressing one of two keys on a keyboard which correspond to "Yes" and "No". Measurements of accuracy (i.e., did participants select the correct key) and response time (how quickly they pressed the key in milliseconds) can therefore be taken as response measurements.

The Emoji Spatial Stroop task can be easily modified for other research purposes. For example, we are currently testing horizontal space-valence effects (left versus right), and this can extend to undertaking replications of the Simon effect (Simon & Rudell, 1967), but with emoji stimuli. These can be operationalised to test a variety of valence-space affordances and their relationship to how emotion concepts are retrieved in respect of emoji stimuli.

Lexical and Semantic Decision Tasks

Chapter 2 included a review of research that has studied how emoji may function as an aid to semantic and/or lexical processing. A key methodological paradigm to test these effects are semantic or lexical decision tasks. Semantic categorisation tasks require participants to make a decision in respect of classifying stimuli based on its shared meaning with other stimuli options. Alternatively, lexical decision tasks are concerned with the "wordness" of the stimuli. Experiments utilising this approach typically include a series of trials in which participants are presented with a stimulus in the form of a string of letters which is either a word or a non-word. They are simply asked to make a decision on whether or not the stimulus is a word (Yes or No). To be able to perform this task effectively, the semantic representation of the target needs to be activated, and thus evidenced through accurate categorisation. In respect of affective relations (which is arguably of more relevance to emoji as stimuli), tasks such as the lexical decision task have been adapted to manipulate the valence of the stimuli to ascertain affective categorisation effects (Fazio, 2001; Fazio et al., 1986)

Studies in line with this have observed processing advantages that emotion-laden words may hold over neutral ones. That is, in respect of lexical processing, emotional valence impacts the processing of visual stimuli (Kuchinke et al., 2005; Lane et al., 1999). Specifically, positively or negatively laden stimuli tend to show processing advantages relative to neutral stimuli (Citron et al., 2014; Kousta et al., 2009; Ponari et al., 2015), whereby they tend to be responded to more accurately and quickly. Importantly, these effects appear to be relevant both to stimuli that represent emotion (e.g., words depicting an emotional state) as well as emotion-laden words (e.g., words with emotional associations) (Vinson et al., 2014). Word stimuli are typically manipulated to include positively and negatively valenced words (e.g., "victory" and "death", respectively) and neutral words. Outcome measures consist of the accuracy of responses (i.e., did participants correctly identify that the stimulus presented was a word or not) and the response time to issue this decision.

For emoji, the main principles of the lexical decision task can be applied but rather than asking "Is this a word?", the instructions can be adapted to "Is this a human face?" (Kaye et al., 2021). As such, stimuli vary between being images of human faces and emoji (with valence manipulated equally within these). Studies that have specifically tested emoji in this regard have broadly been concerned with understanding whether there are equivalent processing advantages for emotionally valenced emoji (e.g., happy or sad emoji) relative to neutral ones. Our recent studies have suggested that this might not be the case. That is, when using implicit responses via the lexical decision task on emoji stimuli varying in valence, we have not observed any significant differences in people's accuracy or latency of their responses, indicating that there are no specific processing advantages for more valenced emoji (Kaye et al., 2021, 2023). See Fig. 4.1 for a visual summary of these findings.

This raises the question of the extent to which the valence assumed to be expressed in emoji is quite as evident or influential as what might be typically found in word counterparts. It is conceivably the case that focusing on valence may be a flawed approach here, and instead, a more exclusive focus on manipulating specific emotion depictions within emoji stimuli might elicit alternative effects in such a categorisation task. Additionally, an alternative approach when using the lexical decision task in the study of emoji might be to manipulate other features of emoji stimuli to establish whether there may be other sensori-perceptual features of emoji (e.g., arousal, dominance, etc) which might support categorisation using this task.

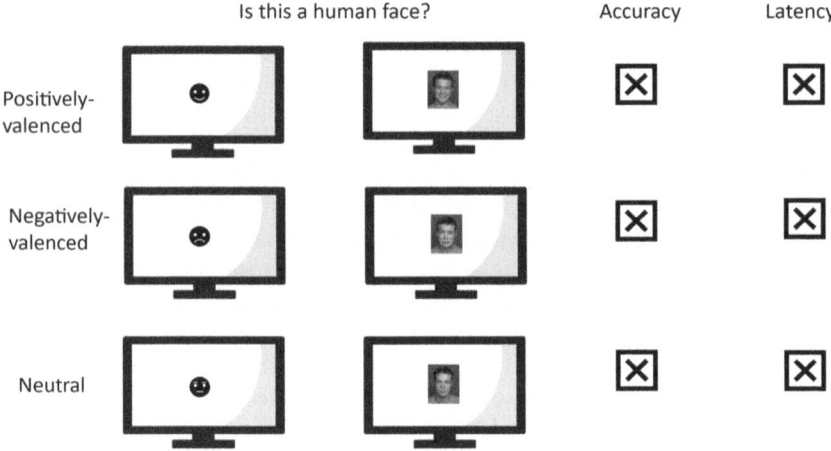

Fig. 4.1 Visual summary of emoji valence in a categorisation task

Dot Probe Task

The Dot Probe task can implicitly measure attentional vigilance to stimuli. This can therefore help answer questions such as how stimuli denoting social threat (e.g., angry or fearful expressions) might be afforded vigilance over neutral stimuli. In the case of emoji, this can present useful insight into the extent to which these social threats are afforded to emoji as stimuli and thus contribute to discussions about whether they are best considered as "emotional" stimuli from the receiver's perspective.

The Dot Probe task is a computerised task whereby participants are presented with a threat cue and a neutral cue. This is immediately followed by a short interval in which a target cue replaces one of the original ones (Bar-Haim et al., 2007; MacLeod et al., 1986). These target cues vary between being congruent or incongruent. Specifically, congruent ones consist of the target cue being presented in the location previously occupied by the threat cue. Conversely, incongruent trials consist of the target appearing in the location previously occupied by the neutral cue. The task measures participants' response times to the target stimulus whereby attentional bias to "threat" is evidenced by faster key press response times when the target occupies congruent relative to incongruent locations. See Fig. 4.2 for an example trial structure of the Dot Probe task.

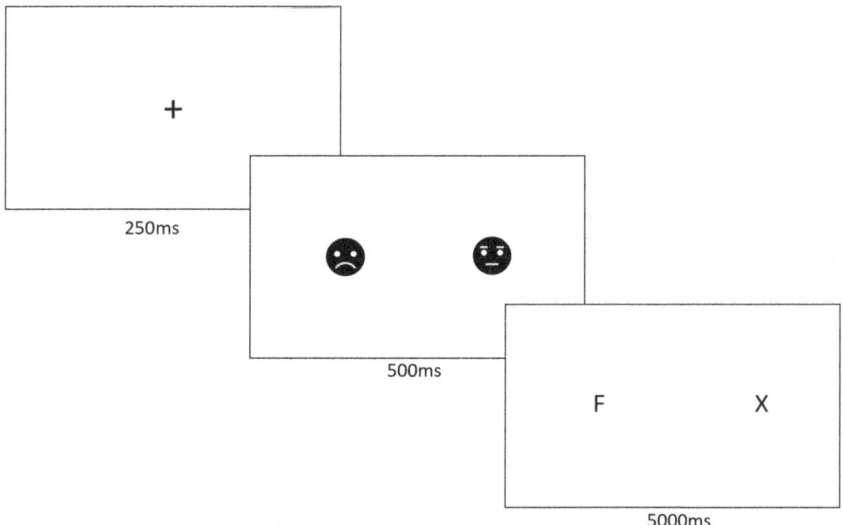

Fig. 4.2 Trial structure of the Dot Probe task

Research utilising this task has shown that we show attentional vigilance to various types of threat-relevant stimuli, including angry and fearful faces (Bocanegra et al., 2012; Cooper & Langton, 2006) and "scary" animals such as spiders or snakes (Lipp & Derakshan, 2005). In the case of emoji, some research has demonstrated that the Dot Probe task captures attentional vigilance to sad emoji for those experiencing depressive symptoms (Wong et al., 2021). However, our own research found no direct evidence that negative-laden emoji (e.g., those depicting sad expressions) elicit attentional vigilance relative to neutral or positive-valenced emoji (MacKenzie et al., 2024). As such, this is suggestive that expressions depicted in emoji might not be processed in equivalent ways to those on faces, and as such, might not be processed as emotional stimuli from the receiver's point of view.

Eye-Tracking

Particularly in relation to the cognitive aspects of processing, the use of eye-tracking can be considered a useful implicit measure of attentional vigilance to specific areas/regions of interest (e.g., specific facial features, target words in sentences) or eye movement patterns, which might signal speed or duration of processing. With knowledge about what visual information is being attended to (and for how long), this can help us make inferences about processes that might be occurring within this. In respect of emoji research, eye-tracking has been used to broadly understand what function emoji play in the lexical, syntactic and/or semantic processes of sentences. However, as noted in Chap. 2, eye tracking could also be used to measure the extent to which we use holistic or featural face processing when encoding emoji, and how this moves toward emotion detection.

Within sentence reading, eye movement behaviour and reaction times can help us explore the visual decoding process which might be taking place (Rayner, 1998). For example, how quickly the eye moves from being fixated on one word to another might signal the level of difficulty in lexical processing for the reader. As such, emoji might be proposed to be an aid in the local lexical or syntactic processing of sentences/words (Paggio & Tse, 2022) but also serve a more global role in supporting semantic integration within this (Beyersmann et al., 2023). That is, if emoji are symbolic of semantic concepts, then they might be proposed to support semantic access and retrieval aspects involved in the processing of lexical information.

Types of eye movement measures which can be used here include local measures such as duration of single fixation (how long the eye is fixated in an area of interest if this is the only fixation to occur here) and duration of first fixation (how long the eye is fixated initially within an area of interest). However, more global measures can equally be useful such as total sentence reading time (sum of all fixations in an area of interest).

Research using eye-tracking in respect of emoji has found that including emoji in sentence-final positions results in longer fixations on the emoji and overall longer sentence reading time compared to when emoji are in sentence-first positions (Robus et al., 2020). This corresponds to other findings which suggest that sentence-final information tends to result in processing costs (Howman & Filik, 2020), potentially from "wrap-up" effects required for semantic integration and comprehension to occur (Hirotani et al., 2006; Rayner et al., 2000). In respect of valence incongruency (emoji valence being different to sentence valence), other research findings show that participants spend longer fixating on stimuli and greater pupil dilation when in incongruent conditions relative to congruent ones, suggesting more effortful processing (García-Carrión et al., 2024). Additionally, fixation behaviour has also been used to demonstrate that when emoji are used to replace words, this results in greater fixation durations (Paggio & Tse, 2022). However, it is unclear from the literature whether the processing costs which are evidenced here are due to the surface-level decoding that might be associated with emoji, including more complex visual features than words, or whether it is due to the higher-order semantic access and retrieval processes which might underpin this.

In summary, whilst eye movement behaviours can help differentiate attentional patterns based on subtle experimental manipulations (e.g., where an emoji is presented in a sentence etc), we are only able to make inferences rather than draw conclusions about how processing efficiency is related to any underpinning processes.

Approach-Avoidance Tasks (AAT)

As noted in Chap. 2, Reinforcement Sensitivity Theory (RST; Gray, 1982, 1987) outlines the processes involved in behavioural approach and avoidance tendencies. In respect of "approach" tendencies, broadly considered to be handled by the Behavioural Activation System (BAS), research widely uses Approach-Avoidance Tasks (Roefs et al., 2011). These can include tasks such as the Stimulus Response Compatibility (SRC, De Houwer et al., 2001) and the joystick Approach-Avoidance Task (AAT, Rinck & Becker, 2007). These tasks require participants to move stimuli towards (approach) or away (avoidance) from themselves via a joystick. Other derivations of this task have used key presses or smartphone movement behaviour as measurements of these action tendencies (Wiers et al., 2009; Zech et al., 2023). However, the Manikin AAT has been established as being a suitable derivation of this paradigm, which is sensitive enough to capture approach-avoidance tendencies (Krieglmeyer & Deutsch, 2009) despite it not requiring large motor activity to elicit an action response. This comprises a manikin symbol on the display screen and participants are instructed to use the up and down keyboard keys to signal whether the stimuli should be moved towards or away from the manikin, respectively. Congruent trials consist of participants being instructed to move the manikin towards the positive stimuli (approach) and away from the negative stimuli (avoidance). Incongruent trials follow the converse pattern.

Interestingly, these paradigms have not yet been applied to the study of emoji to ascertain whether valence represented in emoji may be processed as rewarding (positively valenced emoji) or non-rewarding (negatively valenced emoji) in the way that we might expect for other emotionally laden stimuli. This might proffer an alternative methodological approach to testing behavioural tendencies in respect of emoji and whether they do indeed represent positive and negative as they are assumed to do.

Go/No-Go Task

Following from the previous section outlining paradigms to explore approach-avoidance tendencies, other paradigms focus more specifically on the mechanisms underpinning the BIS. Specifically, this refers to inhibition and our ability to stop a behavioural response. The Go/No-Go task (Gordon & Caramazza, 1982) is a widely used measure of this mechanism in which participants are typically asked to either respond to a stimulus using a key press (Go) or to withhold a response (No-Go). As such, performance on withholding a key press response is deemed to represent one's inhibitory control ability, and in this case, signal strength of avoidance tendencies.

Some researchers have tested emotional derivations of the Go/No-Go tasks whereby instead of letters or pictures as stimuli, affective stimuli have been used, such as affective words or facial expressions (Hare et al., 2005; Murphy et al., 1999). Results from this research suggest that happy words are responded to more quickly on "Go" trials and sad words on "No-Go" trials (Murphy et al., 1999), but the pattern of responses on "No-Go" trials seems somewhat mixed depending on affective characteristics of the sample (e.g., those with depression or manic depression etc.). In respect of facial expressions, evidence suggests that fearful expressions slow down responses and that people have difficulty inhibiting responses to happy faces (Hare et al., 2005). In respect of emoji, it would be intriguing to test inhibitory abilities in this regard, and specifically, the extent to which negatively valenced emoji are processed as non-rewarding stimuli and thus elicit avoidance-type tendencies.

Neuroimaging

Most research on the topic of emoji, which has adopted neuroimaging tools, has used electroencephalogram (EEG). This measures electrical activity in the brain via electrodes attached to the scalp, located in various positions, based on the specific brain region of interest. Outputs from

EEG typically consist of event-related potentials (ERPs) which indicate the level of activation within the brain region of interest. Table 4.1 outlines some of the more typical ERP components that have been explored and what insights these can bring to our understanding of emoji processing.

Neuroimaging approaches have most typically been applied in respect of understanding the extent to which principles of face processing and semantic processing apply to emoji stimuli. In general, research has tended to compare conditions in which emoji stimuli vary in respect of emoji valence, discrete emotion or concept representation (e.g., depicting concrete versus abstract concepts). As outlined in Chap. 2, although evidence

Table 4.1 ERP response, their observed correlates and insights for emoji processing

ERP response	Typical correlates	Insights for emoji processing
P100 (P1)	(Visual) Stimulus encoding and selective attention. P100's latency and amplitude vary with aspects of selective attention or stimulus encoding. Latency is a measure of stimulus classification speed, and amplitude is proportional to the amount of attentional resources devoted to the task and the degree of information processing required.	How emoji may be neurologically processed equivalently to faces.
P200 (P2)	Higher-order perceptual processing of visual stimuli; modulated by attention.	Semantic classification of emoji in respect of efficiency of conceptual knowledge retrieval.
P300 (P3)	Decision-making; stimulus evaluation or categorisation.	Emoji stimuli evaluation or categorisation.
P600	Syntactic violations, semantic reversal anomalies and semantic integration.	Violations of emoji stimuli when used within sentences (e.g., causing a disruption to syntax of a sentence).
N170	Processing of faces, objects or words; structural encoding of faces; modulated by prediction error.	How structural features of emoji may be neurologically processed equivalently to faces. How emotional expression on emoji affects their categorisation/discrimination.

(continued)

Table 4.1 (continued)

ERP response	Typical correlates	Insights for emoji processing
N200	Executive control	Establishing efficiency (early vs late stage) of processing of emoji stimuli and how akin to face processing. The extent to which an inhibitory response controls mechanism (e.g., cognitive control) might apply to action tendencies associated with (negative) emoji.
N400	Semantic processing of words, and other meaningful/relevant stimuli, sensitivity to inconsistent congruency, semantic relation, etc.	What semantic relations exist between emoji and emotion concepts. Violations of emoji stimuli when used within sentences (e.g., causing disruption to sentence valence or when used incongruently to represent a concept).
LPP (late positive potential)	Emotional processing; sustained attention towards motivationally salient stimuli; modulated by the emotional intensity of a stimulus.	The extent to which emoji are processed as emotional stimuli (e.g., how this might vary based on valence or arousal level of stimuli).

tends to suggest that the neurological processes afforded to emoji might be largely equivalent to their counterparts in faces or words, in general, the findings suggest that these are typically less efficient. As such, this indicates that although equivalency might apply to effectiveness, it does not do so for efficiency.

EXPLICIT RESPONSE MEASURES

The previous sections outlined methodological approaches which measure implicit processing, typically via neurological outputs or reaction time tasks. This section considers explicit measurements which have been used in the study of emoji. These broadly consist of explicit memory retrieval tasks or self-report Likert scales to ascertain attitudes or perceptions afforded to emoji.

Memory Retrieval Tasks

Although some studies have issued reaction time studies as a measure of memory retrieval in respect of emoji (Chatzichristos et al., 2020), most research consists of explicit memory recall tasks. This broadly includes free recall following presentation of stimuli. This has been tested in respect of understanding things such as to what extent emoji are processed visuo-spatially or verbally (Homann et al., 2022), whether semantic congruence of emoji supports memory for emoji (Christofalos et al., 2022) and whether valence of emoji might operate as an affective prime for target word recall (Kaye et al., 2023).

For example, research by Homann et al. (2022) asked participants to verbally recall the label/description of target emojis (and words) following different types of distractions. These distractors included both visual and acoustic distraction tasks, and findings suggested that emoji retrieval was aided by being able to draw on both verbal and visual attentional capacities. Other research has tested conditions which vary the congruence of emoji to word/sentence pairings. In respect of semantic congruence, research has utilised recognition tasks and found higher recognition of emoji when the target emoji appeared alongside congruent rather than incongruent sentences (Christofalos et al., 2022). However, in respect of valence, congruence seems to have less of an effect in terms of memory retrieval. Namely, our research has found no difference in memory recall of words irrespective of whether they were presented as valent-congruent or incongruent with words (Kaye et al., 2023).

It appears then that in respect of explicit memory retrieval tasks, there are mixed findings on the role of emoji. These disparities may be attributed to a number of discrepancies in the nature of the research methodologies across studies. Firstly, this may be a product of the nature of response format, which can vary between verbal recall, text input recall or recognition via key press. Secondly, it may be attributed to what target stimuli is being recalled, as this may be the target emoji itself, or in other cases, words which were accompanying/associated with emoji primes. Finally, mixed findings may be a product of the operation of experimental conditions when testing the effects of congruence. That is, manipulating *semantic* congruence broadly appears to elicit more observed effects than *valence* congruence. As such, when utilising explicit memory-retrieval tasks as a measurement of emoji effects, we should remain vigilant that these may not be sufficiently sensitive to fully capture the processes relevant to the hypothesised effects (if indeed these effects exist at all). It is recommended therefore that researchers make use of additional (implicit) measurements alongside these explicit ones, should there be a methodology of interest.

Perception and Attitude Scales

As noted in Chap. 2, much research on the study of emoji has been concerned with their role in interpersonal communication and relationships. In this respect, a large body of research has used methodologies which are typical in person perception research. This broadly consists of Likert scales asking participants to endorse the extent to which they attribute various characteristics to a person (sender of the message) or a message. Typically, experimental conditions vary in respect of valence congruence between emoji and the accompanying message, or in respect of the information participants receive on the nature of the relationship between sender and receiver (e.g., friends, acquaintances, strangers, romantic relationships etc; Rodrigues et al., 2017). For person characteristics, the research has rather exclusively focused on traits such as warmth, personality (typically the Big-5), likeability, sincerity and trustworthiness (Boutet et al., 2021; Huang et al., 2021; Riordan & Glikson, 2020; Wall et al., 2016; Wang et al., 2023a, b). For perceptions of messages, especially when applied in e-commerce contexts, studies have broadly focused on characteristics such as message clarity, sincerity and trustworthiness (Hand et al., 2022; Huang et al., 2021; Wang et al., 2023a, b).

Taking these findings a step further, other research has considered the implications of how these perceptions might have tangible impacts on attitude or behaviour change. Within a commercial context, insights of this nature can be highly fruitful, particularly when considering the way this might result in enhanced brand reputation or even increased sales. Research has shown, for example, that including emoji in promotional advertisements can increase consumers' purchase intentions (Das et al., 2019) and also generate consumer engagement with brand communications (Casado-Molina et al., 2022).

Across the research utilising the methodological approach of perception/attitude scales, evidence generally finds effects on perceptions based on emoji valence, which is interesting given that valence does not tend to elicit such strong or consistent effects in respect of other conceptual approaches or methodologies. As such, it appears that emoji valence is perhaps bound interpersonally and contextually when eliciting processing effects. In this way, emoji processing appears to take the form of being explicit and conscious/deliberate, revealing that the impact of emoji valence is less about retrieving conceptual knowledge (via associative linking) and more about using valence as a cue within social information processing.

Emoji Sentiment Scales

Several scholars have sought to understand how emoji are related to processing by either measuring people's ratings of affective dimensions of emoji (e.g., emotionality, arousal etc) or developing emoji-based scales, broadly to support more efficient and accessible psychometric measurement. This broadly draws on the assumption that emoji can be representative of an affective experience or its intensity (in the case that emoji are used to replace numbers on a numerical scale).

In respect of affective dimensions, research has typically asked participants to use Likert scales to rate emoji which display discrete emotions on dimensions such as emotionality, arousal and valence (Rodrigues et al., 2018; Was & Hamrick, 2021). Studies have tended to either simply assess ratings from these to explore the extent to which emoji are perceived as affective stimuli or assess how these may vary compared to other affective stimuli, such as emoticons or human faces (Fischer & Herbert, 2021).

Within this sphere, a relatively large amount of focus has been on how emoji can help evaluate emotional responses to food (Deubler & Swaney-Stueve, 2020; Jaeger et al., 2016; Swaney-Stueve et al., 2018; Vidal et al., 2016), be used to indicate degree of endorsement to statements relating to course evaluation (Alismail & Zhang, 2020) or to measure psychosocial responses within healthcare settings, such as perceptions of pain, dental anxiety or patient response outcomes (He et al., 2022; Khatri et al., 2021; Setty et al., 2019; Thompson et al., 2018). However, other research has focused more on the use of emoji-based scales to capture more general affective experiences or well-being (Kaye & Schweiger, 2023; Davies et al., 2022), and also how certain emoji might be able to be used to represent items measuring Big-5 personality traits, particularly around extraversion, emotional stability and agreeableness (Marengo et al., 2017).

Because studies of this nature are concerned with people's perceptions of an experience, these typically capture explicit self-reports garnered through responses on Likert scales. In many cases, the key aims of the research are to establish the validity or utility of such scales for psychometric use, and so broadly correspond emoji-based scales with more traditional counterparts or related constructs to test various types of validity. Findings from this type of research can start to identify how reflective emoji may be of affective constructs (at least from a perceptual point of view), which can go some way towards helping us understand how we experience emoji on an (explicit) affective level. However, the operationalisation of these should be noted. Some scholars highlight that for pain scales, some emoji-based scales are more appropriate than others, as they do not include smiley emoji (Moisset et al., 2022). As such, careful consideration is needed on whether the emoji selected to represent items or scale anchors are indeed conceptually appropriate.

SUMMARY

Research on emoji processing has used a wide range of methodological approaches and measures, which raises some challenges when consolidating the main insights from these. Some take-home observations which do appear to be insightful here however include typical types of emoji conditions used in studies and what type of response format seems to elicit the strongest effects.

In relation to emoji stimuli conditions used in this research, these have predominantly compared either:

- presence versus absence of emoji
- semantic congruence vs incongruence of emoji to sentence/word
- valence congruence vs incongruence of emoji to sentence/word
- discrete emotions represented by emoji (i.e., happy, fear, anger, sadness etc)
- emoji versus other affective stimuli (e.g., faces)

Within this, for studies exploring valence effects, control conditions are not always easily operational. That is, neutral emoji are not readily considered neutral stimuli, and therefore may not be best operationalised as a pure control condition.

In respect of the strength of effects, neurological responses and explicit responses/measures tend to elicit more evidence of emoji effects than implicit behavioural measures (e.g., key presses). Namely, this seems to be the case when testing effects between conditions noted above. However, the more "explicit" the response format, the more inconsistent, divergent or non-uniform responses to emoji tend to be (i.e., perception or interpretation scales tend to elicit less standardised effects associated with emoji). That is, although explicit scales may tend to demonstrate that emoji have some impact on the processing/interpretation being measured, the nature of the response will vary considerably based on factors such as the type of emoji, the context it occurs in, between-person differences and so on. As such, whilst the effects might be more evident, they may be less consistent and predictable in nature, compared to neurological responses which might tend to be more uniform.

References

Alismail, S., & Zhang, H. (2020). Exploring and understanding participants' perceptions of facial emoji likert scales in online surveys: A qualitative study. *ACM Transactions on Social Computing, 3*(2). https://doi.org/10.1145/3382505

Bar-Haim, Y., Lamy, D., Pergamin, L., Bakermans-Kranenburg, M. J., & van IJzendoorn, M. H. (2007). Threat-related attentional bias in anxious and non-anxious individuals: A meta-analytic study. *Psychological Bulletin, 133*(1), 1–24. https://doi.org/10.1037/0033-2909.133.1.1

Beyersmann, E., Wegener, S., & Kemp, N. (2023). That's good news ☺: Semantic congruency effects in emoji processing. *Journal of Media Psychology: Theories, Methods, and Applications, 35*(1), 17–27. https://doi.org/10.1027/1864-1105/a000342

Bocanegra, B. R., Huijding, J., & Zeelenberg, R. (2012). Beyond attentional bias: A perceptual bias in a Dot Probe task. *Emotion, 12*(6), 1362–1366. https://doi.org/10.1037/a0028415

Boutet, I., LeBlanc, M., Chamberland, J. A., & Collin, C. A. (2021). Emojis influence emotional communication, social attributions, and information processing. *Computers in Human Behavior, 119*, 106722. https://doi.org/10.1016/j.chb.2021.106722

Casado-Molina, A. M., Rojas-de Gracia, M. M., Alarcón-Urbistondo, P., & Romero-Charneco, M. (2022). Exploring the opportunities of the emojis in brand communication: The case of the beer industry. *International Journal of Business Communication, 59*(3), 315–333. https://doi.org/10.1177/2329488419832964

Chatzichristos, C., Morante, M., Andreadis, N., Kofidis, E., Kopsinis, Y., & Theodoridis, S. (2020). Emojis influence autobiographical memory retrieval from reading words: An fMRI-based study. *PLoS One, 15*(7), e0234104. https://doi.org/10.1371/journal.pone.0234104

Christofalos, A. L., Feldman, L. B., & Sheridan, H. (2022). Semantic congruency facilitates memory for emojis. In *Proceedings of the fifth international workshop on emoji understanding and applications in social media* (pp. 63–68). Association for Computational Linguistics.

Citron, F. M. M., Gray, M. A., Critchley, H. D., & Weekes, B. S. (2014). Emotional valence and arousal affect reading in an interactive way: Neuroimaging evidence for an approach-withdrawal framework. *Neuropsychologia, 56,* 79–89. https://doi.org/10.1016/j.neuropsychologia.2014.01.002

Cooper, R. M., & Langton, S. R. (2006). Attentional bias to angry faces using the Dot Probe task? It depends when you look for it. *Behaviour Research and Therapy, 44*(9), 1321–1329. https://doi.org/10.1016/j.brat.2005.10.004

Das, G., Wiener, H. J. D., & Kareklas, I. (2019). To emoji or not to emoji? Examining the influence of emoji on consumer reactions to advertising. *Journal of Business Research, 96,* 147–156. https://doi.org/10.1016/j.jbusres.2018.11.007

Davies, J., McKenna, M., Denner, K., Bayley, J., & Morgan, M. (2022). The emoji current mood and experience scale: The development and initial validation of an ultra-brief, literacy independent measure of psychological health. *Journal of Mental Health.*

De Houwer, J., Crombez, G., Baeyens, F., & Hermans, D. (2001). On the generality of the affective Simon effect. *Cognition and Emotion, 15*(2), 189–206. https://doi.org/10.1080/02699930125883

Deubler, G., & Swaney-Stueve, M. (2020). The K-State emoji scale, a cross-cultural validation with adults. *Journal of Sensory Studies, 35*(4), e12573. https://doi.org/10.1111/joss.12573

Fazio, R. H. (2001). On the automatic activation of associated evaluations: An overview. *Cognition and Emotion, 15,* 115–142. https://doi.org/10.1080/02699930125908

Fazio, R. H., Sanbonmatsu, D. M., Powell, M. C., & Kardes, F. R. (1986). On the automatic activation of attitudes. *Journal of Personality and Social Psychology, 50,* 229–238. https://doi.org/10.1037/0022-3514.50.2.229

Fischer, B., & Herbert, C. (2021). Emoji as affective symbols: Affective judgments of emoji, emoticons, and human faces varying in emotional content. *Frontiers in Psychology, 12.* https://doi.org/10.3389/fpsyg.2021.645173

García-Carrión, B., Muñoz-Leiva, F., Del Barrio-García, S., & Porcu, L. (2024). The effect of online message congruence, destination-positioning, and emojis on users' cognitive effort and affective evaluation. *Journal of Destination Marketing & Management, 31,* 100842. https://doi.org/10.1016/j.jdmm.2023.100842

Gordon, B., & Caramazza, A. (1982). Lexical decision for open- and closed-class words: Failure to replicate differential frequency sensitivity. *Brain and Language, 15,* 143–160. https://doi.org/10.1016/0093-934X(82)90053-0

Gray, J. A. (1982). *The neuropsychology of anxiety: An enquiry into the functions of the septo-hippocampal system.* Clarendon Press.

Gray, J. A. (1987). The neuropsychology of emotion and personality. In S. M. Stahl, S. D. Iverson, & E. C. Goodman (Eds.), *Cognitive neurochemistry* (pp. 171–190). Oxford University Press.

Hand, C. J., Burd, K., Oliver, A., & Robus, C. M. (2022). Interactions between text content and emoji types determine perceptions of both messages and senders. *Computers in Human Behavior Reports, 8,* 100242. https://doi.org/10.1016/j.chbr.2022.100242

Hare, T. A., Tottenham, N., Davidson, M. C., Glover, G. H., & Casey, B. J. (2005). Contributions of amygdala and striatal activity in emotion regulation. *Biological Psychiatry, 57*(6), 624–632. https://doi.org/10.1016/j.biopsych.2004.12.038

He, S., Renne, A., Argandykov, D., Convissar, D., & Lee, J. (2022). Comparison of an emoji-based visual analog scale with a numeric rating scale for pain assessment. *JAMA, 328*(2), 208–209. https://doi.org/10.1001/jama.2022.7489

Hirotani, M., Frazier, L., & Rayner, K. (2006). Punctuation and intonation effects on clause and sentence wrap-up: Evidence from eye movements. *Journal of Memory and Language, 54*(3), 425–443. https://doi.org/10.1016/j.jml.2005.12.001

Homann, L. A., Roberts, B. R. T., Ahmed, S., & Fernandes, M. A. (2022). Are emojis processed visuo-spatially or verbally? Evidence for dual codes. *Visual Cognition, 30*(4), 267–279. https://doi.org/10.1080/13506285.2022.2050871

Howman, H. E., & Filik, R. (2020). The role of emoticons in sarcasm comprehension in younger and older adults: Evidence from an eye-tracking experiment. *Quarterly Journal of Experimental Psychology, 73*(11), 1729–1744. https://doi.org/10.1177/1747021820922804

Huang, Y., Ma, J., Wu, C.-H., & Yang, S. (2021). An emoji is worth a thousand words? The influence of face emojis on consumer perceptions of user-generated reviews. *Journal of Global Information Management, 29*(6). https://doi.org/10.4018/JGIM.20211101.oa2

Jaeger, S. R., Vidal, L., Kam, K., & Ares, G. (2016). Can emoji be used as a direct method to measure emotional associations to food names? Preliminary investigations with consumers in USA and China. *Food Quality and Preference, 56,* 38–48.

Kaye, L. K., Darker, G., Rodriguez Cuadrado, S., Wall, H. J., & Malone, S. A. (2022). The Emoji Spatial Stroop task: Exploring the impact of vertical positioning of emoji on emotional processing. *Computers in Human Behavior,* 107267. https://doi.org/10.1016/j.chb.2022.107267

Kaye, L. K., MacKenzie, A. K., Rodriguez-Cuadrado, S., Malone, S. A., Stacey, J., & Garrot, E. (2023). (Not) Feeling up or down?: Lack of evidence for vertical spatial iconicity effects for valence evaluations of emoji stimuli. *Computers in Human Behavior, 149,* 107931. https://doi.org/10.1016/j.chb.2023.107931

Kaye, L. K., Rocabado, J. F., Rodriguez Cuadrado, S., Jones, B. R., Malone, S. A., Wall, H. J., & Duñabeitia, J. A. (2023). Exploring the (lack of) facilitative effect of emoji for emotional word processing. *Computers in Human Behavior, 139*, 107563. https://doi.org/10.1016/j.chb.2022.107563

Kaye, L. K., Rodriguez Cuadrado, S., Malone, S. A., Wall, H. J., Gaunt, E., Mulvey, A. L., & Graham, C. (2021). How emotional are emoji?: Exploring the effect of emotional valence on the processing of emoji stimuli. *Computers in Human Behavior, 116*, 106648.

Kaye, L. K., & Schweiger, C. R. (2023). Are emoji valid indicators of in-the-moment mood? *Computers in Human Behavior, 148*, 107916. https://doi.org/10.1016/j.chb.2023.107916

Khatri, A., Kalra, N., Tyagi, R., Sharma, M., Yangdol, P., & Garg, N. (2021). Evaluation of pain in children using animated emoji scale: A novel self-reporting pain assessment tool. *International Journal of Pedodontic Rehabilitation, 6*(1), 20–24. https://doi.org/10.4103/ijpr.ijpr_39_20

Kousta, S.-T., Vinson, D. P., & Vigliocco, G. (2009). Emotion words, regardless of polarity, have a processing advantage over neutral words. *Cognition, 112*(3), 473–481. https://doi.org/10.1016/j.cognition.2009.06.007

Krieglmeyer, R., & Deutsch, R. (2009). Comparing measures of approach–avoidance behaviour: The manikin task vs. two versions of the joystick task. *Cognition and Emotion, 24*(5), 810–828. https://doi.org/10.1080/02699930903047298

Kuchinke, L., Jacobs, A. M., Grubich, C., Vo, M. L.-H., Conrad, M., & Hermann, M. (2005). Incidental effects of emotional valence in single word processing: An fMRI study. *NeuroImage, 28*(4), 1022–1032. https://doi.org/10.1016/j.neuroimage.2005.06.050

Lane, R. D., Chua, P. M.-L., & Dolan, R. J. (1999). Common effects of emotional valence, arousal and attention on neural activation during visual processing of pictures. *Neuropsychologia, 37*(9), 989–997. https://doi.org/10.1016/S0028-3932(99)00017-2

Lipp, O. V., & Derakshan, N. (2005). Attentional bias to pictures of fear-relevant animals in a Dot Probe task. *Emotion, 5*(3), 365–369. https://doi.org/10.1037/1528-3542.5.3.365

MacKenzie, A. K., Stacey, J. E., Rodriguez-Cuadrado, S., Malone, S. A., Pimprikar, A., & Kaye, L. K. (2024, July 1). *Emoji are not emotional: Evidence from an attention probe task*. [Oral presentation] British Psychological Society's Cyberpsychology Section Annual Conference.

MacLeod, C. M. (1991). Half a century of research on the Stroop effect: An integrative review. *Psychological Bulletin, 109*(2), 163–203. https://doi.org/10.1037/0033-2909.109.2.163

MacLeod, C., Mathews, A., & Tata, P. (1986). Attentional bias in emotional disorders. *Journal of Abnormal Psychology, 95*(1), 15–20. https://doi.org/10.1037/0021-843x.95.1.15

Marengo, D., Giannotta, F., & Settanni, M. (2017). Assessing personality using emoji: An exploratory study. *Personality and Individual Differences, 112,* 74–78. https://doi.org/10.1016/j.paid.2017.02.037

Moisset, X., Attal, N., & Ciampi de Andrade, D. (2022). An emoji-based visual analog scale compared with a numeric rating scale for pain assessment. *JAMA, 328*(19), 1980. https://doi.org/10.1001/jama.2022.16940

Murphy, F. C., Sahakian, B. J., Rubinsztein, J. S., Michael, A., Rogers, R. D., Robbins, T. W., & Paykel, A. S. (1999). Emotional bias and inhibitory control processes in mania and depression. *Psychological Medicine, 29*(6), 1307–1321. https://doi.org/10.1017/S0033291799001233

Novak, P. K., Smailović, J., Sluban, B., & Mozetič, I. (2015). Sentiment of emojis. *PLoS One, 10*(12), e0144296. https://doi.org/10.1371/journal.pone.0144296

Paggio, P., & Tse, A. P. P. (2022). Are emoji processed like words? An eye-tracking study. *Cognitive Science, 46,* e13099. https://doi.org/10.1111/cogs.13099

Ponari, M., Rodríguez-Cuadrado, S., Vinson, D., Fox, N., Costa, A., & Vigliocco, G. (2015). Processing advantage for emotional words in bilingual speakers. *Emotion, 15*(5), 644–652. https://doi.org/10.1037/emo0000061

Rayner, K. (1998). Eye movements in reading and information processing: 20 years of research. *Psychological Bulletin, 124*(3), 372–422. https://doi.org/10.1037/0033-2909.124.3.372

Rayner, K., Kambe, G., & Duffy, S. A. (2000). The effect of clause wrap-up on eye movements during reading. *The Quarterly Journal of Experimental Psychology Section A, 53*(4), 1061–1080. https://doi.org/10.1080/713755934

Rinck, M., & Becker, E. S. (2007). Approach and avoidance in fear of spiders. *Journal of Behavior Therapy and Experimental Psychiatry, 38*(2), 105–120. https://doi.org/10.1016/j.jbtep.2006.10.001

Riordan, M. A., & Glikson, E. (2020). On the hazards of the technology age: How using emojis affects perceptions of leaders. *International Journal of Business Communication.* https://doi.org/10.1177/2329488420971690

Robus, C. M., Hand, C. J., Filik, R., & Pitchford, M. (2020). Investigating effects of emoji on neutral narrative text: Evidence from eye movements and perceived emotional valence. *Computers in Human Behavior, 109,* 106361. https://doi.org/10.1016/j.chb.2020.106361

Rodrigues, D., Lopes, D., Prada, M., Thompson, D., & Garrido, M. V. (2017). A frown emoji can be worth a thousand words: Perceptions of emoji use in text messages exchanged between romantic partners. *Telematics and Informatics, 34*(8), 1532–1543. https://doi.org/10.1016/j.tele.2017.07.001

Rodrigues, D., Prada, M., Gaspar, R., Garrido, M. V., & Lopes, D. (2018). Lisbon Emoji and Emoticon Database (LEED): Norms for emoji and emoticons in seven evaluative dimensions. *Behavior Research Methods, 50*(1), 392–405. https://doi.org/10.3758/s13428-017-0878-6

Roefs, A., Huijding, J., Smulders, F. T. Y., MacLeod, C. M., de Jong, P. J., Wiers, R. W., & Jansen, A. T. M. (2011). Implicit measures of association in psychopathology research. *Psychological Bulletin, 137*(1), 149–193. https://doi.org/10.1037/a0021729

Scarpina, F., & Tagini, S. (2017). The Stroop color and word test. *Frontiers in Psychology, 8,* 557. https://doi.org/10.3389/fpsyg.2017.00557

Setty, J. V., Srinivasan, I., Radhakrishna, S., Melwani, A. M., & Krishna, M. (2019). Use of an animated emoji scale as a novel tool for anxiety assessment in children. *Journal of Dental Anesthesia and Pain Medicine, 19*(4), 227–233. https://doi.org/10.17245/jdapm.2019.19.4.227

Simon, J. R., & Rudell, A. P. (1967). Auditory S-R compatibility: The effect of an irrelevant cue on information processing. *Journal of Applied Psychology, 51,* 300–304. https://doi.org/10.1037/h0020586

socks888. (2023). *Is it just me or the emoji for the "Neutral" emotion looks more sad than neutral?* [Online forum post]. Reddit. https://www.reddit.com/r/finch/comments/12cibuc/is_it_just_me_or_the_emoji_for_the_neutral/

Stroop, J. R. (1935). Studies of interference in serial verbal reactions. *Journal of Experimental Psychology, 18,* 643–662. https://doi.org/10.1037/h0054651

Swaney-Stueve, M., Jepsen, T., & Deubler, G. (2018). The emoji scale: A facial scale for the 21st century. *Food Quality and Preference, 68,* 183–190. https://doi.org/10.1016/j.foodqual.2018.03.002

Thompson, C. A., Novotny, P. J., Bartz, A., Yost, K. J., & Sloan, J. A. (2018). Development of novel emoji scale to measure patient-reported outcomes in cancer patients. *Journal of Clinical Oncology, 36*(7), 174.

Vidal, L., Ares, G., & Jaeger, S. R. (2016). Use of emoticon and emoji in tweets for food-related emotional expression. *Food Quality and Preference, 49,* 119–128.

Vinson, D., Ponari, M., & Vigliocco, G. (2014). How does emotional content affect lexical processing? *Cognition and Emotion, 28*(4), 737–746. https://doi.org/10.1080/02699931.2013.851068

Wall, H. J., Taylor, P. J., & Campbell, C. (2016). Getting the balance right? A mismatch in interaction demands between target and judge impacts on judgement ac curacy for some traits but not others. *Personality and Individual Differences, 88,* 66–72. https://doi.org/10.1016/j.paid.2015.08.037

Wang, X., Cheng, M., Zhu, J., & Jiang, R. (2023a). When texts meet emoji: A multi-stage study of tourism brands. *Journal of Travel Research.* https://doi.org/10.1177/00472875231203396

Wang, K.-Y., Chih, W.-H., & Honora, A. (2023b). How the emoji use in apology messages influences customers' responses in online service recoveries: The moderating role of communication style. *International Journal of Information Management, 69,* 102618. https://doi.org/10.1016/j.ijinfomgt.2022.102618

Was, C. A., & Hamrick, P. (2021). What did they mean by that? Young adults' interpretations of 105 common emojis. *Frontiers in Psychology, 12,* 655297. https://doi.org/10.3389/fpsyg.2021.655297

White, B. W. (1969). Interference in identifying attributes and attribute names. *Perception & Psychophysics, 6,* 166–168. https://doi.org/10.3758/BF032 10086

Wiers, R. W., Rinck, M., Dictus, M., & Wildenberg van den, E. (2009). Relatively strong automatic appetitive action-tendencies in male carriers OPRM1 G-allele. *Genes, Brain and Behavior, 8,* 101–106. https://doi.org/10.1111/j.1601-183X.2008.00454.x

Wong, M.-Y., Lee, C. K., Croarkin, P. E., & Lee, P. F. (2021). A Dot Probe paradigm for attention bias detection in young adults. In F. Ibrahim, J. Usman, M. Y. Ahmad, & N. Hamzah (Eds.), *3rd international conference for innovation in biomedical engineering and life sciences. ICIBEL 2019. IFMBE proceedings* (Vol. 81). Springer. https://doi.org/10.1007/978-3-030-65092-6_18

Wuhr, P. (2007). A Stroop effect for spatial orientation. *The Journal of General Psychology, 134*(3), 285–294. https://doi.org/10.3200/genp.134.3.285-294

Zech, H. G., Gable, P., van Dijk, W. W., & van Dillen, L. F. (2023). Test-retest reliability of a smartphone-based approach-avoidance task: Effects of retest period, stimulus type, and demographics. *Behavior Research Methods, 55,* 2652–2668. https://doi.org/10.3758/s13428-022-01920-6

Conclusion

Abstract Chapter 5 synthesises the key learning and take-home points from the book and articulates an informed judgement about the state of play and future opportunities for the psychological study of emoji processing. This presents the "Emoji Processing Model" and the "Emoji Research Toolkit" as pragmatic resources to help researchers themselves advance the study of emoji processing.

Keywords Emoji • Emotional processing • Interpersonal processing • Cognitive processing • Computer-mediated communication • Research
A key objective behind writing this book was to provide a resource which could extract insights from a range of rather disparate sub-disciplines in psychology to provide a comprehensive review of the state-of-play of what we know about how we process emoji. Within this book, I have consolidated the literature which focuses on emoji processing from the receiver's perspective. This chapter will take forward these insights to synthesise and also provide some recommendations for how this might inform future research priorities or approaches.

L. K. Kaye, *The Psychology of Emoji Processing*, Palgrave Studies in Cyberpsychology, https://doi.org/10.1007/978-3-031-75113-4_5

So How *Are* Emoji Processed?

The short answer is diversely! On a neurological level, emoji appear to hold some universal processing affordances (although these often appear to be "slower" signals than other stimuli counterparts). Specifically, there are unlikely to be variations in how emoji are processed on this level between people. However, when considering how they are processed relative to other stimuli, they may not be entirely equivalent, certainly in terms of efficiency.

Despite there being some uniformity at a neurological level, beyond this, emoji in general are too semantically ambiguous and contextually bound for us to draw universal conclusions about their function or the way they are processed for the receiver. In some cases, they might serve as emotional markers, but also might support semantic or lexical processing, and also serve as social/interpersonal cues. It is equally conceivable that they may concurrently serve any of these combinations of functions at any given instance. The between-person and within-person variations which exist here are extensive, and we should recognise that the most coherent conclusion we can come to is that emoji processing is diverse.

In respect of a synthesis of the literature, Fig. 5.1 presents the Emoji Processing Model which provides a visual representation of this. This extends previous models which discuss distinct pathways of associative

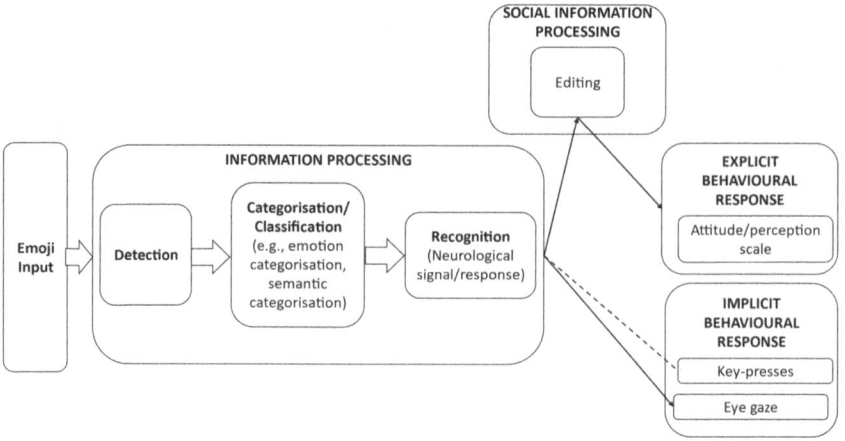

Fig. 5.1   Emoji Processing Model

linking versus propositional reasoning (e.g., Gawronski & Bodenhausen, 2006, 2007). Within the Emoji Processing Model, I draw insights about how these pathways relate to phases of processing and where different measurements of effects (if they exist) may occur within this. In this model, I have noted the implicit phases of processing to refer to "information processing" largely as the majority of the literature which this relates to falls in a domain under such a description. I have then used the term "social information processing" to describe the more explicit, deliberative processing phases which are proposed to occur later in the process. This would correspond to the literature which explores the interpersonal processing aspects of emoji, or in other cases, simply measures the affective dimensions of emoji using explicit, self-report measurements. The lines towards the behaviour response boxes indicate where null effects (dashed line) have typically been observed, relative to evidence of observed effects (bold lines). Effects here are broadly with respect to comparisons between different emoji conditions, as noted in Chap. 4.

In respect of observed effects, speaking in broad terms, neurological signals/responses generally appear to be most uniform and sufficiently sensitive to detect effects associated with dimensions of emoji (e.g., signals associated with emotion recognition, semantic classification etc). Following this, eye gaze as a (implicit) behavioural measure appears to be sufficiently sensitive to signal some discrimination processes in emoji processing (e.g., semantic "wrap-up" in sentences, structural processing). However, when measurements refer to behavioural responses such as key presses (which are said to be ways of measuring implicit responses), this is where we see fewer observed effects, largely represented by null effects within the literature. However, if explicit measurements such as self-report assessments are being used, this is where deliberative processing may start to occur, which benefits from conscious forms of social and interpersonal-based information processing,[1] thus eliciting effects in many cases.

To answer the question about whether there is universality in the processing of emoji, it seems that this might be the case in the early-stage detection/discrimination process via the use of implicit measures (neurological measurements, eye-tracking) but divergence occurs at the point at

---

[1] It is acknowledged that some aspects of social information processing might refer to attributions or biases which are implicit. In these cases, automatic bias activation would be said to occur within the "categorisation/classification" box of the model which would integrate with the implicit information processing phase of the process.

which behavioural responses are initiated and certainly once social information processing starts to feature in the process. Put another way, it appears that it is the point at which "discrimination" becomes "interpretation" when the processing of emoji shifts from being more universal to more divergent. The discrimination processes largely refer to those typical for emotion detection/recognition and semantic categorisation, which occur at the implicit level. However, these either do not translate/transfer to certain types of behavioural responses or the behavioural measures used are not sufficiently sensitive to capture any implicit-based processes. At the point of interpretation, this draws on deliberative processing, which requires greater cognitive resources, such as to issue labels and understand contextual affordances to draw inferences related to emoji stimuli. Within this latter stage, there is more room for divergence and appears to be the point at which processing becomes less uniform and where we see differences at the individual level, but also at the generational and even societal level.

How Does the Literature Help Us Answer Commonly Asked Questions About Emoji?

Based on the literature consolidated within this book, I thought it might be useful to summarise these as responses to frequently asked questions (FAQs). As such, these are my evidence-informed responses drawn from the insights garnered from writing this book.

Q. Is Emoji a Universal Language?
No. There is little evidence to suggest that there are universal interpretations of these. Their interpretation appears to be very much context-dependent. Additionally, there are diversities in the labels we attach to emoji, suggesting that there is little universality in interpretation (and use).

Q. Do Emoji Function Like Facial Expressions?
No. There is not clear or compelling evidence that we detect emotion from emoji equivalently to that of face counterparts. Even in cases when similar activation has been found on a neurological level, the degree and efficiency of this activation appears different for emoji compared to faces. Additionally, there lacks universality on the anatomical presentation of emoji and these do not seem particularly consistent with face counterparts.

Q. Do Emoji Help Us Understand People/Support Relationships?
Yes. Whilst this will vary based on the type of relationship or context they are used in, emoji generally seem to be helpful as interpersonal cues signalling things such as warmth and openness, which can support impression management and positive relationship development.

Q. Do Emoji Represent Mood States?
To some extent, but not universally. Receivers' personality is one characteristic which affects how much association there is between certain emoji and corresponding mood state labels people afford to these.

Q. Do Emoji Represent Emotion Concepts?
No, not at an implicit level. However, our self-reports of emoji suggest that we often associate them towards emotion-relevant labels, although these are not always universally applied. It is important to note that the majority of research on implicit processing has studied this in respect of varying emoji valence using happy, sad and neutral emoji. As such, it would be useful for additional work to test these assertions on a range of other emoji which represents other discrete emotions or explores other dimensional categories beyond valence.

Q. Do Emoji Support Semantic Processing?
Yes, particularly when emoji are in sentence-final positions. Interestingly, valence of emoji (and whether or not this is congruent to word/sentence valence) does not always seem to help or hinder processing or reading of words, but semantic congruency of an emoji to the accompanying text seems to be important.

Q. Can Emoji Replace Words?
Probably not. Replacing words with semantically relevant emoji does not seem to facilitate semantic processing.

FUTURE DIRECTIONS

There have been various points within this book where I have signalled the value of future research enquiries to follow up on specific under-explored research questions or under-exploited approaches and methods. However, for the purposes of a more complete summary, I include these here, as well as other broader ideas for research issues to explore. I list these under the broader conceptually-related approaches in the interests of keeping these coherent to the more general approach taken in this book.

Emotional Functions of Emoji

- *Discrete emotions*—Because a strong focus in the literature has been on the impact of emoji valence, this has somewhat overshadowed a more specific focus on how discrete emotions represented in emoji are processed at various levels. Whilst there has been research within the face processing literature on fear and anger for example, there is perhaps a need for a more exclusive focus on the range of discrete emotions depicted in emoji, and how these function in emotional processing. Within this, applying some of the methodological paradigms outlined in Chap. 4 could advance these conceptual principles further.
- *What is a suitable control condition?*—Whilst it might not be research question itself or indeed exclusive just to the emotional processing domain, it would be interesting for scholars in this field to synthesise how "neutral" emoji or control conditions have been operationalised in various domains in this field. I would anticipate some form of systematic review or meta-analysis could be especially useful to draw out these insights to help researchers in this area have a basis for implementing good practice in this respect.
- *Approach-Avoidance tendencies*—As noted in Chap. 2, future research could adopt paradigms to establish whether approach-avoidance principles apply to positive and negative emotions, respectively, as depicted in emoji. This might advance our understanding of the extent to which we implicitly associate positive emoji to approach-based motivational systems (e.g., BAS) and negative emoji to inhibitory systems (BIS) as might be expected in our typical motivational and/or physiological responses to these emotions.

Cognitive Processing of Emoji

- *Concept representation*—As valence of emoji does not appear to have strong or consistent effects in semantic processing, focusing on more specific emotion depictions or concepts might be more relevant to study in relation to semantic processing. Within this, the concreteness of what concepts emoji are representing seems important and so some further research which tests concrete vs abstract vs emotion concepts as depicted by emoji could be helpful.

- *Superiority effects*—As noted in Chap. 2, the Sensory-Semantic Model proffers an insight into how emoji as images might elicit superiority effects relative to words within the encoding process. Here it might be fruitful to manipulate the complexity or richness of visual features of emoji to understand how this impacts on the effectiveness and/or efficiency of the encoding and semantic retrieval process.
- *Semantic learning*—Whilst a majority of research has focused on the role of emoji in semantic processing, comprehension and retrieval, much less has been focused on the encoding and learning of concepts. Therefore, research which explores how novel concepts can be learnt through exposure or semantic priming with referent emoji could be an intriguing avenue to pursue.
- *Sensorimotor affordances*—As noted in Chap. 2, exploring the sensorimotor affordances of emoji might offer a more nuanced and multidimensional way to understand the way we process emoji. Normative data on this might help advance our ability to go beyond more basic features (e.g., valence, concreteness) when identifying emoji for experimental conditions. Sensorimotor affordances associated with emoji also help situate emoji work in the more general field of grounded cognition/embodied cognition, which is helpful when making claims about the significance of findings. Finally, understanding the richer sensory experiences associated with emoji gives us more insight into the potential richness of these within the context of online communication, which is often assumed to be impoverish.

Interpersonal Processing of Emoji

- Because the way we use and interpret emoji is largely contextually and interpersonally bound, it is pertinent to consider how this shapes emoji conceptualisation and behaviour. Namely, as noted in Chap. 3, the role of perspective-taking here is pertinent and might function as a way of helping dyads/interaction partners create shared concepts of what certain emoji represent, and therefore engage in adaptive communication. As such, some research which explores how shared concept representation develops in the case of emoji and the role of perspective-taking or constructs such as Theory of Mind within this process would be really intriguing.

Emoji Research Toolkit

Figure 5.2 presents the Emoji Research Toolkit. This is designed as a pragmatic tool for researchers in this area to develop research questions which are coherently aligned with theoretical frameworks and methodologies. This has been informed by the insights derived from consolidating and synthesising the available literature on emoji processing.

I hope that this presents you with a helpful synthesis of the emoji processing literature and can form a strong basis for any empirical endeavours you might choose to pursue on this fascinating topic!

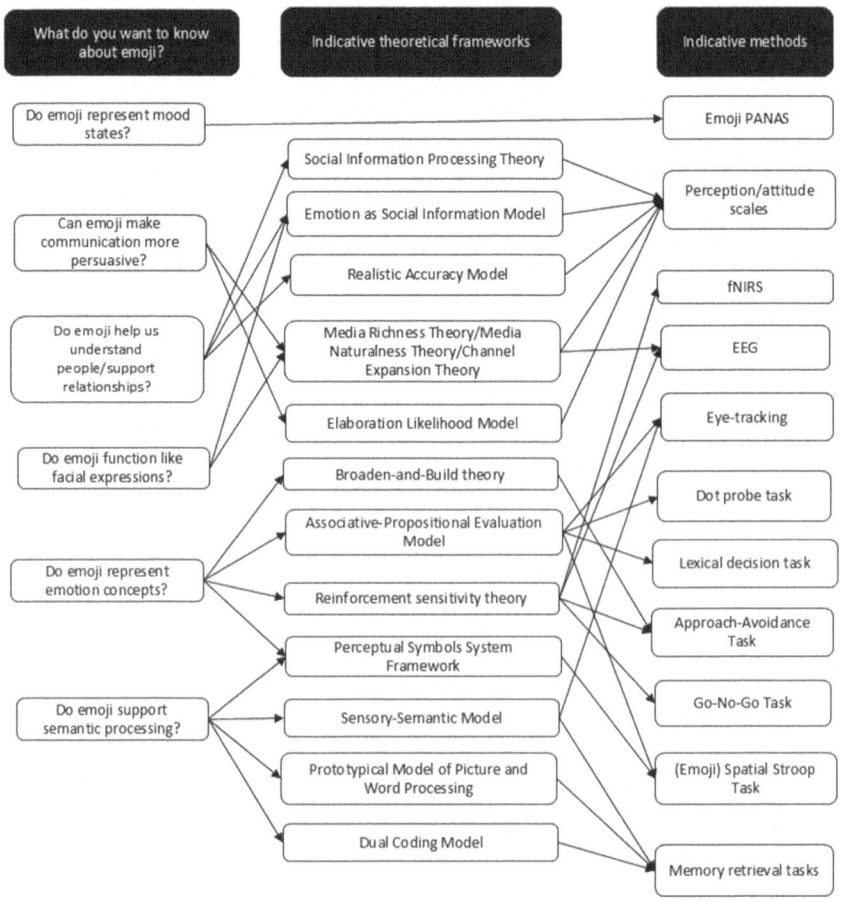

Fig. 5.2   Emoji Researcher Toolkit

REFERENCES

Gawronski, B., & Bodenhausen, G. V. (2006). Associative and propositional processes in evaluation: An integrative review of implicit and explicit attitude change. *Psychological Bulletin, 132,* 692–731. https://doi.org/10.1037/0033-2909.132.5.692

Gawronski, B., & Bodenhausen, G. V. (2007). Unraveling the processes underlying evaluation: Attitudes from the perspective of the APE model. *Social Cognition, 25,* 687–717.

REFERENCES

Aldunate, N., & González-Ibáñez, R. (2017). An integrated review of emoticons in computer-mediated communication. *Frontiers in Psychology, 7*, 1–6. https://doi.org/10.3389/fpsyg.2016.02061

Aldunate, N., Villena-González, M., Rojas-Thomas, F., López, V., & Bosman, C. A. (2018). Mood detection in ambiguous messages: The interaction between text and emoticons. *Frontiers in Psychology, 9.* https://doi.org/10.3389/fpsyg.2018.00423

Alismail, S., & Zhang, H. (2020). Exploring and understanding participants' perceptions of facial emoji likert scales in online surveys: A qualitative study. *ACM Transactions on Social Computing, 3*(2). https://doi.org/10.1145/3382505

Aluja, A., Balada, F., Blanco, E., Lucas, I., & Blanch, A. (2020). Startle reflex modulation by affective face "Emoji" pictographs. *Psychological Research, 84*, 15–22. https://doi.org/10.1007/s00426-018-0991-x

Atkinson, R. C., & Shiffrin, R. M. (1971). The control of short term memory. *Scientific American, 225*(2), 82–90. https://doi.org/10.1038/scientificamerican0871-82

Barach, E., Feldman, L. B., & Sheridan, H. (2021). Are emojis processed like words?: Eye movements reveal the time course of semantic processing for emojified text. *Psychonomic Bulletin Review, 28*, 978–991. https://doi.org/10.3758/s13423-020-01864-y

Bar-Haim, Y., Lamy, D., Pergamin, L., Bakermans-Kranenburg, M. J., & van IJzendoorn, M. H. (2007). Threat-related attentional bias in anxious and non-anxious individuals: A meta-analytic study. *Psychological Bulletin, 133*(1), 1–24. https://doi.org/10.1037/0033-2909.133.1.1

© The Author(s), under exclusive license to Springer Nature
Switzerland AG 2024
L. K. Kaye, *The Psychology of Emoji Processing*, Palgrave
Studies in Cyberpsychology,
https://doi.org/10.1007/978-3-031-75113-4

Barrett, L. F. (2006). Are emotions natural kinds? *Perspectives on Psychological Science, 1*(1), 28–58. https://doi.org/10.1111/j.1745-6916.2006.00003.x

Barsalou, L. W. (1999). Perceptual symbol systems. *Behavioral and Brain Sciences, 22*, 577–660. https://doi.org/10.1017/s0140525x99002149

Batson, C. D., Shaw, L. L., & Oleson, K. C. (1992). Differentiating affect, mood, and emotion: Toward functionally based conceptual distinctions. In M. S. Clark (Ed.), *Emotion* (pp. 294–326). Sage Publications.

Beedie, C., Terry, P., & Lane, A. (2005). Distinctions between emotion and mood. *Cognition and Emotion, 19*(6), 847–878. https://doi.org/10.1080/02699930541000057

Beyersmann, E., Wegener, S., & Kemp, N. (2023). That's good news ☺: Semantic congruency effects in emoji processing. *Journal of Media Psychology: Theories, Methods, and Applications, 35*(1), 17–27. https://doi.org/10.1027/1864-1105/a000342

Bocanegra, B. R., Huijding, J., & Zeelenberg, R. (2012). Beyond attentional bias: A perceptual bias in a Dot Probe task. *Emotion, 12*(6), 1362–1366. https://doi.org/10.1037/a0028415

Bocanegra, B. R., & Zeelenberg, R. (2011). Emotional cues enhance the attentional effects on spatial and temporal resolution. *Psychonomic Bulletin & Review, 18*(6), 1071–1076. https://doi.org/10.3758/s13423-011-0156-

Boutet, I., LeBlanc, M., Chamberland, J. A., & Collin, C. A. (2021). Emojis influence emotional communication, social attributions, and information processing. *Computers in Human Behavior, 119*, 106722. https://doi.org/10.1016/j.chb.2021.106722

Bradley, M. M., Greenwald, M. K., Petry, M. C., & Lang, P. J. (1992). Remembering pictures: Pleasure and arousal in memory. *Journal of Experimental Psychology. Learning, Memory, and Cognition, 18*(2), 379–390. https://doi.org/10.1037/0278-7393.18.2.379

Butterworth, S. E., Giuliano, T. A., White, J., Cantu, L., & Fraser, K. C. (2019). Sender gender influences emoji interpretation in text messages. *Frontiers in Psychology, 10*. https://doi.org/10.3389/fpsyg.2019.00784

Calvo, M., Avero, P., & Lundqvist, D. (2006). Facilitated detection of angry faces: Initial orienting and processing efficiency. *Cognition and Emotion, 20*(6), 785–811. https://doi.org/10.1080/02699930500465224

Calvo, M. G., & Nummenmaa, L. (2008). Detection of emotional faces: Salient physical features guide effective visual search. *Journal of Experimental Psychology: General, 137*(3), 471–494. https://doi.org/10.1037/a0012771

Carlson, J. R., & Zmud, R. W. (1999). Channel expansion theory and the experiential nature of media richness perceptions. *Academy of Management Journal, 42*(2), 153–170. https://doi.org/10.2307/257090

Casado-Molina, A. M., Rojas-de Gracia, M. M., Alarcón-Urbistondo, P., & Romero-Charneco, M. (2022). Exploring the opportunities of the emojis in brand communication: The case of the beer industry. *International Journal of Business Communication, 59*(3), 315–333. https://doi.org/10.1177/2329488419832964

Cavalheiro, B. P., Prada, M., & Rodrigues, D. L. (2024). Examining the effects of reciprocal emoji use on interpersonal and communication outcomes. *Journal of Social and Personal Relationships, 41*(8), 2147–2168. https://doi.org/10.1177/02654075231219

Cavalheiro, B. P., Prada, M., & Rodrigues, D. L. (n.d.). *Show yourself?! Social presence as a mechanism for the effects of using different pictorial cues in text-based computer-mediated communication.*

Cavalheiro, B. P., Prada, M., Rodrigues, D. L., Garrido, M. V., & Lopes, D. (2022). With or without Emoji? Perceptions about emoji use in different brand-consumer communication contexts. *Human Behavior and Emerging Technologies, 2022*, 3036664. https://doi.org/10.1155/2022/3036664

Chatzichristos, C., Morante, M., Andreadis, N., Kofidis, E., Kopsinis, Y., & Theodoridis, S. (2020). Emojis influence autobiographical memory retrieval from reading words: An fMRI-based study. *PLoS One, 15*(7), e0234104. https://doi.org/10.1371/journal.pone.0234104

Childers, T. L., & Houston, M. J. (1983). Imagery paradigms for consumer research: Alternative perspectives from cognitive psychology. In R. P. Bagozzi & A. M. Tybout (Eds.), *Advances in consumer research* (pp. 59–64). Association for Consumer Research.

Christofalos, A. L., Feldman, L. B., & Sheridan, H. (2022). Semantic congruency facilitates memory for emojis. In *Proceedings of the fifth international workshop on emoji understanding and applications in social media* (pp. 63–68). Association for Computational Linguistics.

Citron, F. M. M., Gray, M. A., Critchley, H. D., & Weekes, B. S. (2014). Emotional valence and arousal affect reading in an interactive way: Neuroimaging evidence for an approach-withdrawal framework. *Neuropsychologia, 56*, 79–89. https://doi.org/10.1016/j.neuropsychologia.2014.01.002

Clark, A. (1998). *Being there: Putting brain, body, and world together again.* MIT Press.

Connell, L., & Lynott, D. (2012). Strength of perceptual experience predicts word processing performance better than concreteness or imageability. *Cognition, 125*(3), 452–465. https://doi.org/10.1016/j.cognition.2012.07.010

Connell, L., Lynott, D., & Dreyer, F. (2012). A functional role for modality-specific perceptual systems in conceptual representations. *PLoS One, 7*(3), e33321. https://doi.org/10.1371/journal.pone.0033321

Cooper, R. M., & Langton, S. R. (2006). Attentional bias to angry faces using the Dot Probe task? It depends when you look for it. *Behaviour Research and Therapy, 44*(9), 1321–1329. https://doi.org/10.1016/j.brat.2005.10.004

Coyle, M. A., & Carmichael, C. L. (2019). Perceived responsiveness in text messaging: The role of emoji use. *Computers in Human Behavior, 99,* 181–189. https://doi.org/10.1016/j.chb.2019.05.023

Craik, F. I. M., & Lockhart, R. S. (1972). Levels of processing: A framework for memory research. *Journal of Verbal Learning and Verbal Behavior, 11*(6), 671–684. https://doi.org/10.1016/S0022-5371(72)80001-X

D'Argembeau, A., & Van der Linden, M. (2011). Influence of facial expressions on memory for facial identity: Effects of visual features on emotional meaning. *Emotion, 11*(1), 199–202. https://doi.org/10.1037/a0022592

D'Urso, S. C. (2020). Channel expansion theory. In J. Bulck (Ed.), *The international encyclopedia of media psychology* (1st ed., pp. 1–6). Wiley. https://doi.org/10.1002/9781119011071.iemp0119

Daft, R. L., & Lengel, R. H. (1986). Organizational information requirements, media richness and structural design. *Management Science, 32*(5), 554–571. https://doi.org/10.1287/mnsc.32.5.554

Daft, R. L., Lengel, R. H., & Trevino, L. K. (1987). Message equivocality, media selection, and manager performance: Implications for information systems. *MIS Quarterly, 11*(3), 355–366. https://doi.org/10.2307/248682

Danesi, M. (2017). *The semiotics of emoji: The rise of visual language in the age of the internet.* Bloomsbury Publishing.

Darbyshire, D. E., Kirk, C., Wall, H. J., & Kaye, L. K. (2016). Don't judge a (Face)Book by its cover: Exploring judgement accuracy of others' personality on Facebook. *Computers in Human Behavior, 58,* 380–387. https://doi.org/10.1016/j.chb.2016.01.021

Das, G., Wiener, H. J. D., & Kareklas, I. (2019). To emoji or not to emoji? Examining the influence of emoji on consumer reactions to advertising. *Journal of Business Research, 96,* 147–156. https://doi.org/10.1016/j.jbusres.2018.11.007

Davies, J., McKenna, M., Denner, K., Bayley, J., & Morgan, M. (2024). The emoji current mood and experience scale: The development and initial validation of an ultra-brief, literacy independent measure of psychological health. *Journal of Mental Health, 33*(2), 218–226. https://doi.org/10.1080/09638237.2022.2069694

De Houwer, J., Crombez, G., Baeyens, F., & Hermans, D. (2001). On the generality of the affective Simon effect. *Cognition and Emotion, 15*(2), 189–206. https://doi.org/10.1080/02699930125883

de la Vega, I., de Filippis, M., Lachmair, M., Dudschig, C., & Kaup, B. (2012). Emotional valence and physical space: Limits of interaction. *Journal of Experimental Psychology: Human Perception and Performance, 38*(2), 375–385. https://doi.org/10.1037/a0024979

de la Vega, I., Dudschig, C., De Filippis, M., Lachmair, M., & Kaup, B. (2013). Keep your hands crossed: The valence-by-left/right interaction is related to hand, not side, in an incongruent hand–response key assignment. *Acta Psychologica, 142*(2), 273–277. https://doi.org/10.1016/j.actpsy.2012.12.011

Derks, D., Bos, A. E. R., & Von Grumbkow, J. (2008a). Emoticons and online message interpretation. *Social Science Computer Review, 26*(3), 379–388. https://doi.org/10.1177/0894439307311611

Derks, D., Fischer, A. H., & Bos, A. E. R. (2008b). The role of emotion in computer-mediated communication: A review. *Computers in Human Behavior, 24*(3), 766–785. https://doi.org/10.1016/j.chb.2007.04.004

Deubler, G., & Swaney-Stueve, M. (2020). The K-State emoji scale, a cross-cultural validation with adults. *Journal of Sensory Studies, 35*(4), e12573. https://doi.org/10.1111/joss.12573

Distel, V., Egger, R., Petrovic, U., Phan, V. L., & Wiesinger, S. (2022). The usage of emoji in tourism-related Instagram posts: Suggestions from a marketing perspective. In J. L. Stienmetz, B. Ferrer-Rosell, & D. Massimo (Eds.), *Information and communication technologies in tourism 2022. Proceedings of the ENTER 2022 eTourism conference.* Springer.

Dudscig, C., de la Vega, I., & Kaup, B. (2015). What's up? Emotion-specific activation of vertical space during language processing. *Acta Psychologica, 156*, 143–155. https://doi.org/10.1016/j.actpsy.2014.09.015

Eastwood, J. D., Smilek, D., & Merikle, P. M. (2001). Differential attentional guidance by unattended faces expressing positive and negative emotion. *Perception & Psychophysics, 63*(6), 1004–1013. https://doi.org/10.3758/bf03194519

Eisenberger, N. I., & Cole, S. W. (2012). Social neuroscience and health: Neurophysiological mechanisms linking social ties with physical health. *Nature Neuroscience, 15*(5), 669–674. https://doi.org/10.1038/nn.3086

Ekman, P., & Rosenberg, E. (1997). *What the face reveals: Basic and applied studies of spontaneous expression using the facial action coding system (FACS).* Oxford University Press.

Fazio, R. H. (2001). On the automatic activation of associated evaluations: An overview. *Cognition and Emotion, 15*, 115–142. https://doi.org/10.1080/02699930125908

Fazio, R. H., Sanbonmatsu, D. M., Powell, M. C., & Kardes, F. R. (1986). On the automatic activation of attitudes. *Journal of Personality and Social Psychology, 50*, 229–238. https://doi.org/10.1037/0022-3514.50.2.229

Feldman Barrett, L., & Russell, J. A. (1998). The structure of current affect: Controversies and emerging consensus. *Current Directions in Psychological Science, 8*, 10–14. https://doi.org/10.1111/1467-8721.000

Fischer, B., & Herbert, C. (2021). Emoji as affective symbols: Affective judgments of emoji, emoticons, and human faces varying in emotional content. *Frontiers in Psychology, 12.* https://doi.org/10.3389/fpsyg.2021.645173

Fisher, S. (1964). Depressive affect and perception of up-down. *Journal of Psychiatric Research, 2,* 25–30. https://doi.org/10.1176/appi.psychotherapy.1965.19.1.172

Fredrickson, B. L. (1998). What good are positive emotions? *Review of General Psychology, 2,* 300–319. https://doi.org/10.1037/1089-2680.2.3.300

Fredrickson, B. L. (2001). The role of positive emotions in positive psychology. The broaden-and-build theory of positive emotions. *American Psychologist, 56*(3), 218–226. https://doi.org/10.1037/0003-066x.56.3.218

Fugate, J. M. B., & Franco, C. L. (2021). Implications for emotion: Using anatomically based facial coding to compare emoji faces across platforms. *Frontiers in Psychology, 12.* https://doi.org/10.3389/fpsyg.2021.605928

Fullwood, C., & Martino, O. I. (2007). Emoticons and impression formation. *Applied Semiotics, 19*(8), 4–14.

Funder, D. C. (1995). On the accuracy of personality judgment: A realistic approach. *Psychological Review, 102*(4), 652. https://doi.org/10.1037/0033-295x.102.4.652

Funder, D. C. (1999). *Personality judgment: A realistic approach to person perception.* Academic Press.

Gantiva, C., Araujo, A., Castillo, K., Claor, L., & Hurtado-Parrado, C. (2021). Physiological and affective responses to emoji faces: Effects on facial muscle activity, skin conductance, heart rate, and self-reported affect. *Biological Psychology, 163,* 108142. https://doi.org/10.1016/j.biopsycho.2021.108142

Gantiva, C., Sotaquirá, M., Araujo, A., & Cuervo, P. (2020). Cortical processing of human and emoji faces: An ERP analysis. *Behaviour & Information Technology, 39*(8), 935–943. https://doi.org/10.1080/0144929X.2019.1632933-

García-Carrión, B., Muñoz-Leiva, F., Del Barrio-García, S., & Porcu, L. (2024). The effect of online message congruence, destination-positioning, and emojis on users' cognitive effort and affective evaluation. *Journal of Destination Marketing & Management, 31,* 100842. https://doi.org/10.1016/j.jdmm.2023.100842

Gawronski, B., & Bodenhausen, G. V. (2006). Associative and propositional processes in evaluation: An integrative review of implicit and explicit attitude change. *Psychological Bulletin, 132,* 692–731. https://doi.org/10.1037/0033-2909.132.5.692

Gawronski, B., & Bodenhausen, G. V. (2007). Unraveling the processes underlying evaluation: Attitudes from the perspective of the APE model. *Social Cognition, 25,* 687–717. https://doi.org/10.1521/soco.2007.25.5.687

Gawronski, B., & Bodenhausen, G. V. (2009). Operating principles versus operating conditions in the distinction between associative and propositional processes. *Behavioral and Brain Sciences, 32,* 183–246. https://doi.org/10.1017/S0140525X09000855

Gawronski, B., & Bodenhausen, G. V. (2011). The Associative–Propositional evaluation model: Theory, evidence, and open questions. *Advances in Experimental Social Psychology, 44,* 59–127. https://doi.org/10.1016/B978-0-12-385522-0.00002-0

Gentner, D., & Goldin-Meadows, S. (Eds.). (2003). *Language in mind.* MIT Press.

George, A. S., Hovan George, A. S., & Baskar, T. (2023). Emoji unite: Examining the rise of emoji as an international language bridging cultural and generational divides. *Partners Universal International Innovation Journal, 1*(4), 183–204. https://doi.org/10.5281/zenodo.8280356

Gesselman, A. N., Ta-Johnson, V. P., & Garcia, J. R. (2019). Worth a thousand interpersonal words: Emoji as affective signals for relationship-oriented digital communication. *PLoS One, 14*(8), e0221297. https://doi.org/10.1371/journal.pone.0221297

Gibson, J. J. (1979). *The ecological approach to perception.* Lawrence Erlbaum Associates.

Gordon, B., & Caramazza, A. (1982). Lexical decision for open- and closed-class words: Failure to replicate differential frequency sensitivity. *Brain and Language, 15,* 143–160. https://doi.org/10.1016/0093-934X(82)90053-0

Gray, J. A. (1982). *The neuropsychology of anxiety: An enquiry into the functions of the septo-hippocampal system.* Clarendon Press.

Gray, J. A. (1987). The neuropsychology of emotion and personality. In S. M. Stahl, S. D. Iverson, & E. C. Goodman (Eds.), *Cognitive neurochemistry* (pp. 171–190). Oxford University Press.

Hand, C. J., Burd, K., Oliver, A., & Robus, C. M. (2022). Interactions between text content and emoji types determine perceptions of both messages and senders. *Computers in Human Behavior Reports, 8,* 100242. https://doi.org/10.1016/j.chbr.2022.100242

Hand, C. J., Kennedy, A., Filik, R., Pitchford, M., & Robus, C. M. (2023). Emoji identification and emoji effects on sentence emotionality in ASD-diagnosed adults and neurotypical controls. *Journal of Autism and Developmental Disorders, 53*(6), 2514–2528. https://doi.org/10.1007/s10803-022-05557-4)

Hantula, D. A., Kock, N., D'Arcy, J. P., & DeRosa, D. M. (2011). Media compensation theory: A Darwinian perspective on adaptation to electronic communication and collaboration. In G. Saad (Ed.), *Evolutionary psychology in the business sciences* (pp. 339–363). Springer. https://doi.org/10.1007/978-3-540-92784-6_13

Hare, T. A., Tottenham, N., Davidson, M. C., Glover, G. H., & Casey, B. J. (2005). Contributions of amygdala and striatal activity in emotion regulation. *Biological Psychiatry, 57*(6), 624–632. https://doi.org/10.1016/j.biopsych.2004.12.038

He, S., Renne, A., Argandykov, D., Convissar, D., & Lee, J. (2022). Comparison of an emoji-based visual analog scale with a numeric rating scale for pain assessment. *JAMA, 328*(2), 208–209. https://doi.org/10.1001/jama.2022.7489

Hirotani, M., Frazier, L., & Rayner, K. (2006). Punctuation and intonation effects on clause and sentence wrap-up: Evidence from eye movements. *Journal of Memory and Language, 54*(3), 425–443. https://doi.org/10.1016/j.jml.2005.12.001

Homann, L. A., Roberts, B. R. T., Ahmed, S., & Fernandes, M. A. (2022). Are emojis processed visuo-spatially or verbally? Evidence for dual codes. *Visual Cognition, 30*(4), 267–279. https://doi.org/10.1080/13506285.2022.2050871

Howman, H. E., & Filik, R. (2020). The role of emoticons in sarcasm comprehension in younger and older adults: Evidence from an eye-tracking experiment. *Quarterly Journal of Experimental Psychology, 73*(11), 1729–1744. https://doi.org/10.1177/1747021820922804

Huang, Y., Ma, J., Wu, C.-H., & Yang, S. (2021). An emoji is worth a thousand words? The influence of face emojis on consumer perceptions of user-generated reviews. *Journal of Global Information Management, 29*(6), 264–286. https://doi.org/10.4018/JGIM.20211101.oa2

Intraub, H., & Nicklos, S. (1985). Levels of processing and picture memory: The physical superiority effect. *Journal of Experimental Psychology. Learning, Memory, and Cognition, 11*, 284–298. https://doi.org/10.1037/0278-7393.11.2.284

Jaeger, S. R., Vidal, L., Kam, K., & Ares, G. (2016). Can emoji be used as a direct method to measure emotional associations to food names? Preliminary investigations with consumers in USA and China. *Food Quality and Preference, 56*, 38–48. https://doi.org/10.1016/j.foodqual.2016.09.005

Kahneman, D. (2011). *Thinking, fast and slow.* Farrar, Straus and Giroux.

Kaye, L. K., Darker, G., Rodriguez Cuadrado, S., Wall, H. J., & Malone, S. A. (2022a). The Emoji Spatial Stroop Task: Exploring the impact of vertical positioning of emoji on emotional processing. *Computers in Human Behavior, 132*, 107267. https://doi.org/10.1016/j.chb.2022.107267

Kaye, L. K., MacKenzie, A. K., Rodriguez-Cuadrado, S., Malone, S. A., Stacey, J., & Garrot, E. (2023a). (Not) Feeling up or down?: Lack of evidence for vertical spatial iconicity effects for valence evaluations of emoji stimuli. *Computers in Human Behavior, 149*, 107931. https://doi.org/10.1016/j.chb.2023.107931

Kaye, L. K., Malone, S. A., & Wall, H. J. (2017). Emojis: Insights, affordances and possibilities for psychological science. *Trends in Cognitive Sciences, 21*(2), 66–68. https://doi.org/10.1016/j.tics.2016.10.007

Kaye, L. K., Rocabado, J. F., Rodriguez Cuadrado, S., Jones, B. R., Malone, S. A., Wall, H. J., & Duñabeitia, J. A. (2023b). Exploring the (lack of) facilitative effect of emoji for emotional word processing. *Computers in Human Behavior,* *139,* 107563. https://doi.org/10.1016/j.chb.2022.107563

Kaye, L. K., Rodriguez Cuadrado, S., Malone, S. A., Wall, H. J., Gaunt, E., Mulvey, A. L., & Graham, C. (2021). How emotional are emoji?: Exploring the effect of emotional valence on the processing of emoji stimuli. *Computers in Human Behavior, 116,* 106648. https://doi.org/10.1016/j.chb.2020.106648

Kaye, L. K., Rousaki, A., Joyner, L. C., Barrett, L. A. F., & Orchard, L. J. (2022b). The online behaviour taxonomy: A conceptual framework to understand behaviour in computer-mediated communication. *Computers in Human Behavior, 137,* 107443. https://doi.org/10.1016/j.chb.2022.107443

Kaye, L. K., & Schweiger, C. R. (2023). Are emoji valid indicators of in-the-moment mood? *Computers in Human Behavior, 148,* 107916. https://doi.org/10.1016/j.chb.2023.107916

Kaye, L. K., Wall, H. J., & Hird, A. T. (2020). Less is more when rating extraversion: Behavioural cues and interpersonal perceptions on the platform of Facebook. *Psychology of Popular Media, 9*(4), 465–474. https://doi.org/10.1037/ppm0000263

Kendall, L. N., Raffaelli, Q., Kingstone, A., & Todd, R. M. (2016). Iconic faces are not real faces: Enhanced emotion detection and altered neural processing as faces become more iconic. *Cognitive Research: Principles and Implications, 1*(19). https://doi.org/10.1186/s41235-016-0021-8

Ketai, R. (1975). Affect, mood, emotion, and feeling: Semantic considerations. *The American Journal of Psychiatry, 132*(11), 1215–1217. https://doi.org/10.1176/ajp.132.11.1215

Khatri, A., Kalra, N., Tyagi, R., Sharma, M., Yangdol, P., & Garg, N. (2021). Evaluation of pain in children using animated emoji scale: A novel self-reporting pain assessment tool. *International Journal of Pedodontic Rehabilitation, 6*(1), 20–24. https://doi.org/10.4103/ijpr.ijpr_39_20

Kock, N. (2004). The psychobiological model: Towards a new theory of computer-mediated communication based on Darwinian evolution. *Organization Science, 15*(3), 327–348. https://doi.org/10.1287/orsc.1040.0071

Kock, N. (2005). Media richness or media naturalness? The evolution of our biological communication apparatus and its influence on our behavior toward E-communication tools. *IEEE Transactions on Professional Communication, 48*(2), 117–130. https://doi.org/10.1109/TPC.2005.849649

Kock, N. (2011). Media naturalness theory: Human evolution and behaviour towards electronic communication technologies. In S. C. Roberts (Ed.), *Applied evolutionary psychology* (pp. 380–398). Oxford University Press. https://doi.org/10.1093/acprof:oso/9780199586073.003.0023

Kousta, S.-T., Vinson, D. P., & Vigliocco, G. (2009). Emotion words, regardless of polarity, have a processing advantage over neutral words. *Cognition, 112*(3), 473–481. https://doi.org/10.1016/j.cognition.2009.06.007

Kovecses, Z. (2000). *Metaphor and emotion*. Cambridge University Press.

Krieglmeyer, R., & Deutsch, R. (2009). Comparing measures of approach–avoidance behaviour: The manikin task vs. two versions of the joystick task. *Cognition and Emotion, 24*(5), 810–828. https://doi.org/10.1080/02699930903047298

Kuchinke, L., Jacobs, A. M., Grubich, C., Vo, M. L.-H., Conrad, M., & Hermann, M. (2005). Incidental effects of emotional valence in single word processing: An fMRI study. *NeuroImage, 28*(4), 1022–1032. https://doi.org/10.1016/j.neuroimage.2005.06.050

Kumar, R. (1997). The role of affect in negotiations: An integrative overview. *The Journal of Applied Behavioral Science, 33*, 84–100. https://doi.org/10.1177/0021886397331007

Lakoff, G., & Johnson, M. (1980). *Metaphors we live by*. University of Chicago Press.

Lane, R. D., Chua, P. M.-L., & Dolan, R. J. (1999). Common effects of emotional valence, arousal and attention on neural activation during visual processing of pictures. *Neuropsychologia, 37*(9), 989–997. https://doi.org/10.1016/S0028-3932(99)00017-2

Lang, P. J. (1995). The emotion probe: Studies of motivation and attention. *American Psychologist, 50*(5), 372–385. https://doi.org/10.1037/0003-066X.50.5.372

Lang, P. J., Bradley, M. M., & Cuthbert, B. N. (1990). Emotion, attention, and the startle reflex. *Psychological Review, 97*(3), 377–395. https://doi.org/10.1037/0033-295X.97.3.377

Lang, P. J., Bradley, M. M., & Cuthbert, B. N. (1997). Motivated attention: Affect, activation, and action. In P. J. Lang, R. F. Simons, & M. T. Balaban (Eds.), *Attention and orienting: Sensory and motivational processes* (pp. 97–135). Erlbaum.

Larsen, R. J., Mercer, K. A., Balota, D. A., & Strube, M. J. (2008). Not all negative words slow down lexical decision and naming speed: Importance of word arousal. *Emotion, 8*, 445–452. https://doi.org/10.1037/1528-3542.8.4.445

Letzring, T. D., Wells, S. M., & Funder, D. C. (2006). Information quantity and quality affect the realistic accuracy of personality judgment. *Journal of Personality and Social Psychology, 91*(1), 111–123. https://doi.org/10.1037/0022-3514.91.1.111

Liao, W., Zhang, Y., Huang, X., Xu, X., & Peng, X. (2021). "Emoji, I can feel your pain" – Neural responses to facial and emoji expressions of pain. *Biological Psychology, 163*, 108134. https://doi.org/10.1016/j.biopsycho.2021.108134

Lipp, O. V., & Derakshan, N. (2005). Attentional bias to pictures of fear-relevant animals in a Dot Probe task. *Emotion, 5*(3), 365–369. https://doi.org/10.1037/1528-3542.5.3.365

Liu, C. H., Chen, W., & Ward, J. (2014). Remembering faces with emotional expressions. *Frontiers in Psychology, 5*, 1439. https://doi.org/10.3389/psyg.2014.01439

Lu, C. H., & Proctor, R. W. (1995). The influence of irrelevant location information on performance: A review of the Simon and spatial Stroop effects. *Psychonomic Bulletin & Review, 2*(2), 174–207. https://doi.org/10.3758/BF03210959

Lynott, D., Connell, L., Brysbaert, M., Brand, J., & Carney, J. (2020). The Lancaster Sensorimotor Norms: Multidimensional measures of perceptual and action strength for 40,000 English words. *Behavior Research Methods, 52*, 1271–1291. https://doi.org/10.3758/s13428-019-01316-z

MacKenzie, A. K., Stacey, J. E., Rodriguez-Cuadrado, S., Malone, S. A., Pimprikar, A., & Kaye, L. K. (2024, July 1). *Emoji are not emotional: Evidence from an attention probe task.* [Oral presentation] British Psychological Society's Cyberpsychology Section Annual Conference.

MacLeod, C. M. (1991). Half a century of research on the Stroop effect: An integrative review. *Psychological Bulletin, 109*(2), 163–203. https://doi.org/10.1037/0033-2909.109.2.163

MacLeod, C., Mathews, A., & Tata, P. (1986). Attentional bias in emotional disorders. *Journal of Abnormal Psychology, 95*(1), 15–20. https://doi.org/10.1037/0021-843x.95.1.15

Mahon, B. Z. (2015). The burden of embodied cognition. *Canadian Journal of Experimental Psychology, 69*, 172–178. https://doi.org/10.1037/cep0000060

Mahon, B. Z., & Caramazza, A. (2008). A critical look at the embodied cognition hypothesis and a new proposal for grounding conceptual content. *Journal of Physiology, Paris, 102*, 59–70. https://doi.org/10.1016/j.jphysparis.2008.03.004

Marengo, D., Giannotta, F., & Settanni, M. (2017). Assessing personality using emoji: An exploratory study. *Personality and Individual Differences, 112*, 74–78. https://doi.org/10.1016/j.paid.2017.02.037

McShane, L., Pancer, E., Poole, M., & Deng, Q. (2021). Emoji, playfulness, and brand engagement on twitter. *Journal of Interactive Marketing, 53*(1), 96–110. https://doi.org/10.1016/j.intmar.2020.06.002

Meier, B. P., & Robinson, M. D. (2004). Why the sunny side is up: Associations between affect and vertical position. *Psychological Science, 15*(4), 243–247. https://doi.org/10.1111/j.0956-7976.2004.00659.x

Meteyard, L., Rodriguez-Cuadrado, S., Bahrami, B., & Vigliocco, G. (2012). Coming of age: A review of embodiment and the neuroscience of semantics. *Cortex, 48*(7), 788–804. https://doi.org/10.1016/j.cortex.2010.11.002

Michalak, J., Troje, N. F., Fischer, J., Vollmar, P., Heidenreich, T., & Schulte, D. (2009). Embodiment of sadness and depression—Gait patterns associated with dysphoric mood. *Psychosomatic Medicine, 71*(5), 580–587. https://doi.org/10.1097/PSY.0b013e3181a2515c

Miller, H., Thebault-Spieker, J., Chang, S., Johnson, I., Terveen, L., & Hecht, B. (2021). "Blissfully Happy" or "Ready to Fight": Varying interpretations of emoji. *Proceedings of the International AAAI Conference on Web and Social Media, 10*(1), 259–268. https://doi.org/10.1609/icwsm.v10i1.14757

Moisset, X., Attal, N., & Ciampi de Andrade, D. (2022). An emoji-based visual analog scale compared with a numeric rating scale for pain assessment. *JAMA, 328*(19), 1980. https://doi.org/10.1001/jama.2022.16940

Murphy, F. C., Sahakian, B. J., Rubinsztein, J. S., Michael, A., Rogers, R. D., Robbins, T. W., & Paykel, A. S. (1999). Emotional bias and inhibitory control processes in mania and depression. *Psychological Medicine, 29*(6), 1307–1321. https://doi.org/10.1017/S0033291799001233

Neel, L. A. G., McKechnie, J. G., Robus, C. M., & Hand, C. J. (2023). Emoji alter the perception of emotion in affectively neutral text messages. *Journal of Nonverbal Behavior, 47*, 83–97. https://doi.org/10.1007/s10919-022-00421-6

Nelson, D. L. (1979). Remembering pictures and words: Appearance, significance, and name. In L. S. Cermak & F. I. M. Craik (Eds.), *Levels of processing in human memory* (pp. 45–76). Erlbaum.

Nelson, D. L., Reed, V. S., & McEvoy, C. L. (1977). Learning to order pictures and words: A model of sensory and semantic encoding. *Journal of Experimental Psychology: Human Learning and Memory, 3*, 485–497. https://doi.org/10.1037/0278-7393.3.5.485

Nelson, D. L., Reed, V. S., & Walling, J. R. (1976). The pictorial superiority effect. *Journal of Experimental Psychology: Human Learning and Memory, 9*, 523–578. https://doi.org/10.1037/0278-7393.2.5.523

Novak, P. K., Smailović, J., Sluban, B., & Mozetič, I. (2015). Sentiment of emojis. *PLoS One, 10*(12), e0144296. https://doi.org/10.1371/journal.pone.0144296

Öhman, A., Lundqvist, D., & Esteves, F. (2001). The face in the crowd revisited: A threat advantage with schematic stimuli. *Journal of Personality and Social Psychology, 80*(3), 381–396. https://doi.org/10.1037/0022-3514.80.3.381

Ostarek, M., & Vigliocco, G. (2017). Reading sky and seeing a cloud: On the relevance of events for perceptual simulation. *Journal of Experimental Psychology: Learning, Memory, and Cognition, 43*(4), 579–590. https://doi.org/10.1037/xlm0000318

Paggio, P., & Tse, A. P. P. (2022). Are emoji processed like words? An eye-tracking study. *Cognitive Science, 46*, e13099. https://doi.org/10.1111/cogs.13099

Paivio, A. (1969). Mental imagery in associative learning and memory. *Psychological Review, 76*, 241–263.

Paivio, A. (1971). *Imagery and verbal processes.* Holt, Rinehart and Winston.

Paivio, A. & Csapo, K. (1973). Picture superiority in free recall: Imagery or dual coding? *Cognitive Psychology, 5*(2), 176–206. https://doi.org/10.1016/0010-0285(73)90032-7

Paivio, A., & Kelman, C. (1973). Picture superiority in free recall: Imagery or dual coding. *Cognitive Psychology, 5*, 176–906. https://doi.org/10.1016/0010-0285(73)90032-7

Palef, S. R., & Olson, D. R. (1975). Spatial and verbal rivalry in a Stroop-like task. *Canadian Journal of Psychology, 29*(3), 201–209. https://doi.org/10.1037/h0082026

Petty, R. E., & Cacioppo, J. T. (1986). The elaboration likelihood model of persuasion . *Advances in Experimental Social Psychology, 9*, 123–205. https://doi.org/10.1016/S0065-2601(08)60214-2

Pfeifer, V. A., Armstrong, E. L., & Lai, V. T. (2022). Do all facial emojis communicate emotion? The impact of facial emojis on perceived sender emotion and text processing. *Computers in Human Behavior, 126*, 107016. https://doi.org/10.1016/j.chb.2021.107016

Ponari, M., Rodríguez-Cuadrado, S., Vinson, D., Fox, N., Costa, A., & Vigliocco, G. (2015). Processing advantage for emotional words in bilingual speakers. *Emotion, 15*(5), 644–652. https://doi.org/10.1037/emo0000061

Prada, M., Saraiva, M., Cruz, S., Xavier, S., & Rodrigues, D. L. (2022). Using emoji in response to customer reservation requests and service reviews. *Human Behavior and Emerging Technologies, 2022*, 1433055. https://doi.org/10.1155/2022/1433055

Ray, E. C., & Merle, P. F. (2021). Disgusting face, disease-ridden place?: Emoji influence on the interpretation of restaurant inspection reports. *Health Communication, 36*(14), 1867–1878. https://doi.org/10.1080/10410236.2020.1802867

Rayner, K. (1998). Eye movements in reading and information processing: 20 years of research. *Psychological Bulletin, 124*(3), 372–422. https://doi.org/10.1037/0033-2909.124.3.372

Rayner, K., Kambe, G., & Duffy, S. A. (2000). The effect of clause wrap-up on eye movements during reading. *The Quarterly Journal of Experimental Psychology Section A, 53*(4), 1061–1080. https://doi.org/10.1080/713755934

Rinck, M., & Becker, E. S. (2007). Approach and avoidance in fear of spiders. *Journal of Behavior Therapy and Experimental Psychiatry, 38*(2), 105–120. https://doi.org/10.1016/j.jbtep.2006.10.001

Riordan, M. A., & Glikson, E. (2020). On the hazards of the technology age: How using emojis affects perceptions of leaders. *International Journal of Business Communication.* https://doi.org/10.1177/2329488420971690

Robus, C. M., Hand, C. J., Filik, R., & Pitchford, M. (2020). Investigating effects of emoji on neutral narrative text: Evidence from eye movements and perceived emotional valence. *Computers in Human Behavior, 109,* 106361. https://doi.org/10.1016/j.chb.2020.106361

Rodrigues, D., Lopes, D., Prada, M., Thompson, D., & Garrido, M. V. (2017). A frown emoji can be worth a thousand words: Perceptions of emoji use in text messages exchanged between romantic partners. *Telematics and Informatics, 34*(8), 1532–1543. https://doi.org/10.1016/j.tele.2017.07.001

Rodrigues, D., Prada, M., Gaspar, R., Garrido, M. V., & Lopes, D. (2018). Lisbon Emoji and Emoticon Database (LEED): Norms for emoji and emoticons in seven evaluative dimensions. *Behavior Research Methods, 50*(1), 392–405. https://doi.org/10.3758/s13428-017-0878-6

Roefs, A., Huijding, J., Smulders, F. T. Y., MacLeod, C. M., de Jong, P. J., Wiers, R. W., & Jansen, A. T. M. (2011). Implicit measures of association in psychopathology research. *Psychological Bulletin, 137*(1), 149–193. https://doi.org/10.1037/a0021729

Russell, J. A. (2003). Core affect and the psychological construction of emotion. *Psychological Review, 110*(1), 145–172. https://doi.org/10.1037/0033-295X.110.1.145

Scarpina, F., & Tagini, S. (2017). The Stroop color and word test. *Frontiers in Psychology, 8,* 557. https://doi.org/10.3389/fpsyg.2017.00557

Šetić, M., & Domijan, D. (2007). The influence of vertical spatial orientation on property verification. *Language & Cognitive Processes, 22,* 297–312. https://doi.org/10.1080/01690960600732430

Setty, J. V., Srinivasan, I., Radhakrishna, S., Melwani, A. M., & Krishna, M. (2019). Use of an animated emoji scale as a novel tool for anxiety assessment in children. *Journal of Dental Anesthesia and Pain Medicine, 19*(4), 227–233. https://doi.org/10.17245/jdapm.2019.19.4.227

Sheer, V. C., & Chen, L. (2004). Improving media richness theory: A study of interaction goals, message valence, and task complexity in manager-subordinate communication. *Management Communication Quarterly, 18*(1), 76–93. https://doi.org/10.1177/0893318904265803

Simon, J. R., & Rudell, A. P. (1967). Auditory S-R compatibility: The effect of an irrelevant cue on information processing. *Journal of Applied Psychology, 51,* 300–304. https://doi.org/10.1037/h0020586

Smith, M. C., & Magee, L. E. (1980). Tracing the time course of picture – Word processing. *Journal of Experimental Psychology: General, 109,* 373–392. https://doi.org/10.1037/0096-3445.109.4.373

Snodgrass, J. G. (1980). Towards a model for picture and word processing. In P. A. Kolers, M. E. Wrolstad, & H. Bouma (Eds.), *Processing of visible language. Nato conference series* (Vol. 13). Springer. https://doi.org/10.1007/978-1-4684-1068-6_42

Snodgrass, J. G., & Asieghi, A. (1977). The pictorial superiority effect in recognition memory. *Bulletin of the Psychonomic Society, 10*, 1–4. https://doi.org/10.3758/BF03333530

socks888. (2023). *Is it just me or the emoji for the "Neutral" emotion looks more sad than neutral?* [Online forum post]. Reddit. https://www.reddit.com/r/finch/comments/12cibuc/is_it_just_me_or_the_emoji_for_the_neutral/

Stroop, J. R. (1935). Studies of interference in serial verbal reactions. *Journal of Experimental Psychology, 18*, 643–662. https://doi.org/10.1037/h0054651

Swaney-Stueve, M., Jepsen, T., & Deubler, G. (2018). The emoji scale: A facial scale for the 21st century. *Food Quality and Preference, 68*, 183–190. https://doi.org/10.1016/j.foodqual.2018.03.002

Tanaka, Y., Ishikawa, K., Oyama, T., & Okubo, M. (2022). Face inversion does not affect the reversed congruency effect of gaze. *Psychonomic Bulletin and Review, 30*(3), 974–982. https://doi.org/10.3758/s13423-022-02208-8

Tang, M., Chen, B., Zhao, X., & Zhao, L. (2020). Processing network emojis in Chinese sentence context: An ERP study. *Neuroscience Letters, 722*, 134815. https://doi.org/10.1016/j.neulet.2020.134815

Tang, M., Chen, B., Zhao, X., & Zhao, L. (2024). Semantic and syntactic processing of emojis in sentential intermediate positions. *Cognitive Neurodynamics, 18*, 1743–1752. https://doi.org/10.1007/s11571-023-10037-1

Thompson, C. A., Novotny, P. J., Bartz, A., Yost, K. J., & Sloan, J. A. (2018). Development of novel emoji scale to measure patient-reported outcomes in cancer patients. *Journal of Clinical Oncology, 36*(7), 174. https://doi.org/10.1200/JCO.2018.36.7_suppl.174

Thornton, T., Loetscher, T., Yates, M. J., & Nicholls, M. E. R. (2013). The highs and lows of the interaction between word meaning and space. *Journal of Experimental Psychology, 39*, 964–973. https://doi.org/10.1037/a0030467

Treccani, B., Mulatti, C., Sulpizio, S., & Job, R. (2019). Does perceptual simulation explain spatial effects in word categorization? *Frontiers in Psychology, 10*, e1102. https://doi.org/10.3389/fpsyg.2019.01102

Van Kleef, G. A. (2009). How emotions regulate social life: The Emotions as Social Information (EASI) model. *Current Directions in Psychological Science, 18*(3), 184–188. https://doi.org/10.1111/j.1467-8721.2009.01633.x

Vidal, L., Ares, G., & Jaeger, S. R. (2016). Use of emoticon and emoji in tweets for food-related emotional expression. *Food Quality and Preference, 49*, 119–128. https://doi.org/10.1016/j.foodqual.2015.12.002

Vinson, D., Ponari, M., & Vigliocco, G. (2014). How does emotional content affect lexical processing? *Cognition and Emotion, 28*(4), 737–746. https://doi.org/10.1080/02699931.2013.851068

Wall, H. J., Kaye, L. K., & Malone, S. A. (2016b). An exploration of psychological factors on emoticon usage and implications for judgement accuracy. *Computers in Human Behavior, 62*, 70–78. https://doi.org/10.1016/j.chb.2016.03.040

Wall, H. J., Taylor, P. J., & Campbell, C. (2016a). Getting the balance right? A mismatch in interaction demands between target and judge impacts on judgement ac curacy for some traits but not others. *Personality and Individual Differences*, *88*, 66–72. https://doi.org/10.1016/j.paid.2015.08.037

Walther, J. B. (1992). Interpersonal effects in computer-mediated interaction. *Communication Research*, *19*(1), 52–90. https://doi.org/10.1177/009365092019001003

Walther, J. B. (1996). Computer-mediated communication: Impersonal, interpersonal, and hyperpersonal interaction. *Communication Research*, *23*(1), 3–43. https://doi.org/10.1177/009365096023001001

Walther, J. B., & D'Addario, K. P. (2001). The impacts of emoticons on message interpretation in computer-mediated communication. *Social Science Computer Review*, *19*(3), 324–347. https://doi.org/10.1177/089443930101900307

Wang, X., Cheng, M., Zhu, J., & Jiang, R. (2023a). When texts meet emoji: A multi-stage study of tourism brands. *Journal of Travel Research*, *63*(8), 2062–2077. https://doi.org/10.1177/00472875231203396

Wang, K.-Y., Chih, W.-H., & Honora, A. (2023b). How the emoji use in apology messages influences customers' responses in online service recoveries: The moderating role of communication style. *International Journal of Information Management*, *69*, 102618. https://doi.org/10.1016/j.ijinfomgt.2022.102618

Was, C. A., & Hamrick, P. (2021). What did they mean by that? Young adults' interpretations of 105 common emojis. *Frontiers in Psychology*, *12*, 655297. https://doi.org/10.3389/fpsyg.2021.655297

Watson, D., Clark, L. A., & Tellegen, A. (1988). Development and validation of brief measures of positive and negative affect: The PANAS scales. *Journal of Personality and Social Psychology*, *54*, 1063–1070. https://doi.org/10.1037/0022-3514.54.6.1063

Weiss, M., Gutzeit, J., Rodrigues, J., Mussel, P., & Hewig, J. (2019). Do emojis influence social interactions? Neural and behavioral responses to affective emojis in bargaining situations. *Psychophysiology*, *56*(4), e13321. https://doi.org/10.1111/psyp.13321

Weiss, M., Mussel, P., & Hewig, J. (2020). The value of a real face: Differences between affective faces and emojis in neural processing and their social influence on decision-making. *Social Neuroscience*, *15*(3), 255–268. https://doi.org/10.1080/17470919.2019.1675758

Weissman, B. (2019). Emojis in sentence processing: An electrophysiological approach. In *Companion proceedings of the 2019 world wide web conference (WWW '19)* (pp. 478–479). Association for Computing Machinery. https://doi.org/10.1145/3308560.3316544

Weissman, B., Cohn, N., & Tanner, D. (2024). The electrophysiology of lexical prediction of emoji and text. *Neuropsychologia*, *198*, 108881. https://doi.org/10.1016/j.neuropsychologia.2024.108881

Weissman, B., Engelen, J., Bass, E., & Cohn, N. (2023). The Lexicon of emoji? Conventionality modulates processing of emoji. *Cognitive Science, 47*(4), e13275. https://doi.org/10.1111/cogs.13275

Weissman, B., & Tanner, D. (2018). A strong wink between verbal and emoji-based irony: How the brain processes ironic emojis during language comprehension. *PLoS One, 13*(8), e0201727. https://doi.org/10.1371/journal.pone.0201727

White, B. W. (1969). Interference in identifying attributes and attribute names. *Perception & Psychophysics, 6,* 166–168. https://doi.org/10.3758/BF03210086

Wicke, P., & Bologneis, M. (2020). Emoji-based semantic representations for abstract and concrete concepts. *Cognitive Processing, 21,* 615–635. https://doi.org/10.1007/s10339-020-00971-x

Wiers, R. W., Rinck, M., Dictus, M., & Wildenberg van den, E. (2009). Relatively strong automatic appetitive action-tendencies in male carriers OPRM1 G-allele. *Genes, Brain and Behavior, 8,* 101–106. https://doi.org/10.1111/j.1601-183X.2008.00454.x

Willoughby, J. F., & Lu, S. (2018). Do pictures help tell the story? An experimental test of narrative and emojis in a health text message intervention. *Computers in Human Behavior, 79,* 75–82. https://doi.org/10.1016/j.chb.2017.10.031

Wong, M.-Y., Lee, C. K., Croarkin, P. E., & Lee, P. F. (2021). A Dot Probe paradigm for attention bias detection in young adults. In F. Ibrahim, J. Usman, M. Y. Ahmad, & N. Hamzah (Eds.), *3rd international conference for innovation in biomedical engineering and life sciences. ICIBEL 2019. IFMBE proceedings* (Vol. 81). Springer. https://doi.org/10.1007/978-3-030-65092-6_18

Wuhr, P. (2007). A Stroop effect for spatial orientation. *The Journal of General Psychology, 134*(3), 285–294. https://doi.org/10.3200/genp.134.3.285-294

Yang, J., Yang, Y., Xiu, L., & Yu, G. (2020). Effect of emoji prime on the understanding of emotional words – Evidence from ERPs. *Behaviour & Information Technology, 41*(6), 1313–1322. https://doi.org/10.1080/0144929X.2021.1874050

Yu, L., Xu, Q., Cao, F., Liu, J., Zheng, J., Yang, Y., & Zhang, L. (2022). Emotional violation of faces, emojis, and words: Evidence from N400. *Biological Psychology, 173,* 108405. https://doi.org/10.1016/j.biopsycho.2022.108405

Yue, L. (2022). *"Do you know what I mean?" An intercultural cross-generational study on emoji interpretation.* Doctoral dissertation, Radboud University. https://theses.ubn.ru.nl/items/8a2b2241-9e19-472b-9b31-bcec20415ca3

Zech, H. G., Gable, P., van Dijk, W. W., & van Dillen, L. F. (2023). Test-retest reliability of a smartphone-based approach-avoidance task: Effects of retest period, stimulus type, and demographics. *Behavior Research Methods, 55,* 2652–2668. https://doi.org/10.3758/s13428-022-01920-6

Zhao, J., Meng, Q., An, L., & Wang, Y. (2019). An event-related potential com-
    parison of facial expression processing between cartoon and real faces. *PLoS
    One, 14,* e0198868. https://doi.org/10.1371/journal.pone.019886
Zwaan, R. A., & Yaxley, R. H. (2003). Spatial iconicity affects semantic relatedness
    judgments. *Psychonomic Bulletin & Review, 10*(4), 954–958. https://doi.
    org/10.3758/BF03196557

Index[1]

---

[1] Note: Page numbers followed by 'n' refer to notes.

GPSR Compliance

The European Union's (EU) General Product Safety Regulation (GPSR) is a set of rules that requires consumer products to be safe and our obligations to ensure this.

If you have any concerns about our products, you can contact us on ProductSafety@springernature.com

In case Publisher is established outside the EU, the EU authorized representative is:

Springer Nature Customer Service Center GmbH
Europaplatz 3
69115 Heidelberg, Germany

The manufacturer's authorised representative in the EU is Springer
Nature Customer Service Centre GmbH, Europaplatz 3, 69115 Heidelberg,
Germany. If you have any concerns regarding our products, please
contact ProductSafety@springernature.com

Printed and bound by CPI Group (UK) Ltd, Croydon, CR0 4YY
29/04/2026
02099545-0005